T0301313

Structural Funding and Employment in the European Union

To Kandy

Structural Funding and Employment in the European Union

Financing the Path to Integration

Jeffrey Harrop

University of Bradford

Edward Elgar

Cheltenham, UK • Brookfield, US

Published by
Edward Elgar Publishing Limited
8 Lansdown Place
Cheltenham
Glos GL50 2HU
UK

Edward Elgar Publishing Company
Old Post Road
Brookfield
Vermont 05036
US

British Library Cataloguing in Publication Data
Harrop, Jeffrey
    Structural Funding and Employment in the
    European Union: Financing the Path to
    Integration
    I. Title
    337.142

Library of Congress Cataloguing in Publication Data
Harrop, Jeffrey
    Structural funding and employment in the European Union :
  financing the path to integration / Jeffrey Harrop.
        p. cm.
    Includes bibliographical references and index.
    1. Structural adjustment (Economic policy)—European Union
  countries.   2. European Union countries—Economic policy.
  3. European Union countries—Economic conditions—Regional
  disparities.   4. Labor supply—European Union countries.   I. Title.
  HC240.H3517 1996
  331.13'77'094—dc20   95–21331
                                                CIP

ISBN 1 85898 219 7

Typeset by Manton Typesetters, 5–7 Eastfield Road, Louth, Lincolnshire LN11 7AJ, UK
Printed on FSC approved paper
Printed and bound in Great Britain by Marston Book Services Ltd, Oxfordshire

Contents

Figures

Tables

Abbreviations

The following are the main abbreviations used in this book:

ACP	African, Caribbean and Pacific (countries participating in the Lomé Convention)
AWU	Annual Work Unit
BRITE	Basic Research in Industrial Technologies for Europe
CAP	Common Agricultural Policy
CEC	Commission of the European Communities
CFP	Common Fisheries Policy
CIS	Commonwealth of Independent States (of the former Soviet Union)
CSF	Community Support Framework
DG	Directorate-General of the European Commission
EAGGF	European Agricultural Guidance and Guarantee Fund
EC	European Community (pre-Maastricht)
EC(6)	European Community original six members: Belgium, France, Germany, Italy, Luxembourg and the Netherlands
EC(12)	EC(6) plus: Denmark, Ireland, the UK, Greece, Portugal, Spain
ECB	European Central Bank
ECOSOC	Economic and Social Committee
ECSC	European Coal and Steel Community
ECU	European Currency Unit (a basket of European currencies)
EEC	European Economic Community (later became EC)
EFTA	European Free Trade Association
EIB	European Investment Bank
EIF	European Investment Fund
EMS	European Monetary System
EMU	Economic and Monetary Union
EP	European Parliament

ERDF	European Regional Development Fund
ERM	Exchange Rate Mechanism
ESF	European Social Fund
ESU	European Size Unit
EU	European Union (post-Maastricht)
FIFG	Financial Instrument for Fisheries Guidance
GATT	General Agreement on Tariffs and Trade
GDP	Gross Domestic Product
GFCF	Gross Fixed Capital Formation
GNP	Gross National Product
IDOPs	Integrated Development Operational Programmes
IGC	Inter-governmental Conference
IMPs	Integrated Mediterranean Programmes
INI	Instituto Nacional de Industria
LEADER	Liaison Entre Actions de Développement de l'Economie Rurale
NATO	North Atlantic Treaty Organization
NICs	Newly Industrializing Countries
NUTS	Nomenclature of Territorial Units for Statistics
OECD	Organization for Economic Co-operation and Development
OOPEC	Office for Official Publications of the European Communities
R&D	Research and Development
RETI	Régions Européennes de Tradition Industrielle
SEA	Single European Act
SEM	Single European Market
SMEs	Small- and Medium-Sized Enterprises
STAR	Special Telecommunications Action for Regions
TEC	Training and Enterprise Council
TENs	Trans-European Networks
TGV	Train à Grande Vitesse (French high-speed train)
UNICE	Industrial Confederation of the European Community (Union des Industries de la Communauté Européenne)
VAT	Value Added Tax
WEU	Western European Union
YTS	Youth Training Scheme

Preface

This book on 'Structural Funding and Employment in the European Union' has two main purposes. It enables students who are doing more specialized courses to delve deeper into particular aspects of integration in the European Union. The new term 'European Union' is used interchangeably with that of the European Community, though since the Maastricht Treaty came into effect the term 'EC' is more appropriate to the past and the term 'EU' to the present and future. For students who are increasingly taking up post-graduate courses in European Studies, partly because of the employment benefits perceived from this, there is a shortage of specialist books. Although specific books exist on Regional Economics and Geography, there are relatively few devoted to the growing importance of EU activities via the structural funds. Furthermore, what is usually available is treated separately; for example, there is plenty on agriculture, but not the balanced coverage which this book provides of all structural funds. Students of European Studies increasingly come from a wide disciplinary base, and there is a growing market for a text which will be particularly suited to the types of course with which the writer has experience, such as those at the Universities of Bradford and Greenwich.

Another purpose of this book is to cater for those who are increasingly involved in tapping the use of EU structural funds; for example, those in Local Authorities. The EU is seen as a beneficial pool of financial funds which can be used to alleviate the employment problems of many less favoured areas. It is hoped that this book will therefore prove particularly useful for those in the UK whose job it is to understand and operate the structural funds to benefit their locality.

The author has benefited over the years from many visits to the EC. Especially useful material has been gleaned from the European Investment Bank in Luxembourg, from consultations in Brussels, and consultancy work for Directorate General V of the Commission on the Objective 1 regions which have been created in the UK. I am grateful to the University of Bradford which granted me study leave during semester

1, 1994–95. During that period a wealth of material was used from the European Documentation Centre in Bradford, the University of York Library, the National Lending Library at Boston Spa and a short spell spent at the European Documentation Centre in the University of Malta. In addition, I had many useful discussions with my colleagues in the Department of European Studies, Bradford, especially Professor K. Dyson and Ms M. Holmstedt of the European Briefing Unit, who provided useful insight into this subject. However, the interpretation and views expressed in this book are my own, along with any deficiencies it may contain.

Finally, thanks are due to my wife for the preparation for publication and careful reading of the manuscript.

Jeffrey Harrop

Introduction

The structural funds comprise the European Regional Development Fund, the European Social Fund, the European Agricultural Guidance Fund and the Financial Instrument of Fisheries Guidance. In addition, this book contains coverage of the co-ordination of these funds with the European Coal and Steel Community, the European Investment Bank and the most recent financial instrument of the Cohesion Fund. In the Commission in Brussels, Directorate General XVI is responsible for the ERDF, DG V for the ESF, DG VI for the EAGGF and DG XIV for Fisheries. The current regulations of the structural funds were adopted by the Council of the European Communities in July 1993 and apply to the period 1994–99. Those closely involved with the structural funds will be conversant with their five Objectives, and by the end of this book all readers will be familiar with the use and full meaning of such terms.

Various concerns have led me to write this book. The first is continuingly high unemployment throughout the EU and the need to recognize that dealing with this should take precedence over monetary issues such as EMU and Maastricht convergence criteria. It is economic growth and employment in the real economy which matter most to people. Secondly, my concern is whether the EU is capable of tackling unemployment effectively, especially through the structural funds. Since the EC's foundations were constructed on liberal market principles of competition, with limited intervention, has it subsequently developed a sufficient level of intervention to make inroads into unemployment? It still has a very small budget, with limited redistribution, apart from that provided through the structural funds. Meanwhile, like most organizations it is hampered by its past inheritance, which involves over-preoccupation with a Common Agricultural Policy dominated by guaranteed price expenditure. Are the structural fund resources adequate and commensurate to the problems?

Thirdly, how are the structural funds operated? Are the resources targeted effectively and used efficiently? Are the EAGGF, ERDF and

ESF as complementary as intended? What is the right level of intervention and the implications of this for EU, member state and regional level
relationships? Evidence is drawn mainly from UK experience. The UK
was a major architect of EU regional policy, but now has problems not
just with the CAP, the Common Fisheries Policy and the Social Policy,
but also with a Common Regional Policy since the switch of funds from
the poor to the poorest EU regions after enlargement.

While some of the chapters can be read separately and treated indi-
vidually, readers will gain by following the arguments from one chapter
to the next, thus seeing the book as a whole. The scene is set in Chapter
1 which shows the rationale and logic behind enhanced structural funding to smooth the process of deepening and widening the EU. In the
absence of such expenditure a free market results in intolerable inequalities. These are compounded further by the progression from mi-
cro- to macroeconomic integration. For example, the Maastricht Treaty
leading to Economic and Monetary Union will not only deprive countries of the ability to change their exchange rates, but also remove
separate national currencies. It will also impose a common monetary
policy and common budgetary restraints. It is shown that widening the
EU has increased regional inequalities and future enlargements will
extend these differentials further.

Chapter 2 shows that the macroeconomic background against which
Community policy has to operate has become unfavourable. It is failing
to create new jobs at the same pace as the USA or Japan. Thus unemployment has risen and this can be attributed to a combination of short-
term business fluctuations and a long-term business cycle (Kondratieff
waves). This threatens the maintenance of social and economic cohesion in the EU. The fundamental issue is to reduce the overall problem
of unemployment, and regional unemployment is one dimension of this
to which the structural funds are mainly directed.

In Chapter 3 regional imbalance is analysed, beginning with a distinction between different categories of region. Economic activity tends
to concentrate naturally, mainly in the core regions and new technopole
regions at the expense of peripheral underdeveloped regions and declining industrial regions. Hence intervention is necessary to help weaker
regions both at a national and an EU level. The stronger focus of
funding by the latter towards the peripheral underdeveloped regions has
lessened the attractiveness and benefits to the UK. Despite some economic convergence in performance between member states, there has
been little narrowing in inequalities between regions.

Chapter 4 argues that the EU's main defects arise from its small budget and its limited capacity to redistribute income since it has been concerned chiefly with financing resource allocation. It has been preoccupied with agricultural policy which absorbs most of its expenditure. It is the guarantee expenditure for all farmers which has swamped the structural fund guidance expenditure. Hence it is necessary to see the latter in the broader context of the way the EU has operated the CAP. Despite reforms, these have not resolved the problem. However, at least a new start has been made towards a rural development policy. This acknowledges that guarantee spending has been indiscriminate, and that as agriculture continues to become more capital-intensive such a policy could not maintain employment. The new policy to reduce agricultural prices, to increase direct income transfers and to enhance the role of the structural funds are all steps in the right direction. However, one should not underestimate continuing agricultural difficulties resulting from further enlargement.

Chapter 5 traces the evolution of regional policy through its various phases from the European Coal and Steel Community to the European Economic Community. The latter included the European Investment Bank from its inception to the later creation of the European Regional Development Fund. The chapter pinpoints the improvements in operation through its increased funding, integrating its activities with the other structural funds and its clearer objectives and greater coherence. This has been achieved through switching the emphasis to programmes rather than projects, and through enhanced partnership, involving greater powers for the regions themselves. The stages of structural fund planning at the regional level are outlined, culminating in the Community Support Frameworks. The implications of a Europe of the Regions is then touched upon. The priorities of ERDF funding are outlined, in particular the role attached to infrastructure, especially in Objective 1 regions. Finally, the chapter closes with a coverage of Community Initiatives.

Chapter 6 covers social policy and issues such as labour migration and gender equality, but with attention given mainly to the role played by the ESF. It is argued that whilst expenditure by the ESF to improve the operation of the labour market, for example, through mobility, education and training, is desirable, other elements in EU social policy often conflict with the growth of employment increasing costs to employers.

Some final conclusions about the overall effectiveness of the structural funds are provided in the last chapter.

1. A deeper and a wider union

This chapter examines the main developments in the European Union (EU), showing that the processes of deepening and widening it will necessitate much fuller regional and social policies.

EU INTEGRATION

The growth of intra- and extra-EU trade has contributed to efficiency through areas specializing according to their comparative advantage. Also, at a macroeconomic level, this has been conducive to the growth of employment by raising demand to try to ensure that there would be no return to the destructive protectionism and mass unemployment which characterized the inter-war years. The creation of freer trade took place in two blocs: the European Economic Community (EEC) and the European Free Trade Association (EFTA). Despite some concern over the adverse effects of bloc trade on non-member countries, continued tariff-cutting policies within the General Agreement on Tariffs and Trade (GATT) have helped to maintain a fairly open international trading system.

All areas have potential to benefit from trade by exporting goods which embody their abundant factor of production. Hence trade tends to equalize factor prices. The main concern, though, is that in a completely free market by cumulative advantage there will be winners and losers. Those losing are the areas which face significant structural readjustment. Once one drops neoclassical assumptions of full employment, perfect competition, constant returns to scale and complete mobility of factors of production, then significant regional imbalance is in evidence. Firms in some areas grow and gain from internal and external economies of scale, whilst in other areas firms are laying off labour, which is not automatically reabsorbed into expanding sectors. Workers lack appropriate skills, or the wherewithal to move, and they remain unemployed, often for long periods.

The creation of a Common Market involving not only the free flow of goods, but also the free flow of factors of production, was intended to reinforce factor price equalization. Workers would move out of declining sectors and areas to expanding ones, where they would benefit from higher wages. Meanwhile, in the areas they left, new firms would move in to take advantage of the lower costs of land and labour. Unfortunately, neoclassical analysis breaks down because of wage rigidities caused by trades unions seeking comparable and fair national wage rates which have frustrated this equilibrating process. For example, workers in eastern Germany have sought wages comparable with those in the west, despite much lower levels of productivity. The consequence has been a lower level of productive inward investment than one might have anticipated, with many firms instead preferring to supply from their existing manufacturing base in western Germany. However, given the right kind of incentives, capital can be highly mobile, far more so than labour whose intra-EU mobility has been much lower.

It is recognized, therefore, that reliance on market integration *per se* is insufficient. Integration in the EU has moved significantly from its main initial preoccupation with markets and economic efficiency to recognition of the need to create a Community which is cohesive. This involves concern with equity for those facing unemployment or very low incomes in particular sectors and spatially in the Community. The term 'spatial' may be used to extend beyond its main focus on regional imbalance to encompass the growing urban problems of unemployment and social deprivation.

The battle within the EU, as in most member states, is in establishing the balance between economic efficiency in a market system and the need for greater intervention to hold society together. The EU reflects these tensions and essentially it seems to be recognized that progress must be made on both fronts. The mainspring of the original Treaties leaned more towards markets, reflecting the times of the 1950s and 1960s when we were closer to full employment. Since then, enlargement of the EC in the 1970s and 1980s, and two decades of much higher unemployment, have pushed the Community in a more interventionist direction. Pressure from countries with lower living standards and widespread regional and social disparities have changed the character of the EU and will do so even more in the future.

It will be argued that the emphasis on the creation of the Single Market and the 1992 programme marked a turning point for the Community. As a consequence of this, and some adverse reaction to it from weaker areas, the Community took on board the need for even more active redistributive regional and social policies.

This chapter will proceed to give an account of the deepening of the EU, beginning with the Single European Market (SEM). After that the move onwards from microeconomic integration to macroeconomic integration will be considered in the form of Economic and Monetary Union (EMU). Some other aspects of Maastricht are also touched upon. Finally, the effect of enlargement is examined as a further source of widening regional inequalities.

THE SEM

The SEM (that is, the 1992 programme) aimed to complete the establishment of the original Common Market and also to update it. In completing the original Common Market it was realized that the removal of tariffs had neglected the growth of non-tariff barriers. These were exemplified in particular by widely differing standards which were hampering trade in many industries. These are now being harmonized both by European standardizing bodies and also by acceptance of the principle of mutual recognition: that is, that what is an acceptable product to one country's consumers in terms of health and safety should basically be acceptable to another country's consumers.

The updating is manifested particularly in the extension of the SEM beyond trade in industrial and agricultural products (with any reform of the latter neglected in the 1992 programme) to recognition of the growth in services, the latter traditionally having been highly restricted by national regulations. Thus there was a need to open up competition in such services as transport, banking and insurance, to enable consumers to benefit from better choice and lower prices.

In addition, compared with the early years of the Common Market, there has been a growth in size of the public sector in member state economies. These have often been engaged in preferential purchasing policies. It was recognized in the 1992 programme that if the public sector could be opened up to greater competition throughout the EU, instead of being restricted to national suppliers, then prices could be lowered, providing enhanced value for money from public expenditure.

The consequences of these changes were recognized in the Cecchini Report as leading to beneficial microeconomic gains which would accrue to consumers from greater choice and lower prices. Prices would fall towards the lowest cost supplier, and higher cost suppliers would be forced to compete by increasing their levels of efficiency. They would have to accept some reduction in their profits and also restructure and rationalize their productive activities. There would be significant gains in consumer welfare, one source of which would be through increased economies of scale reaped by larger firms. However, the Cecchini Report has been criticized for its tendency to exaggerate these gains. For example, according to S. Holland (1993), economies of scale in the motor industry in the USA have still not been sufficient to save American companies from Japanese competition. He has argued that economies of scope are of growing significance, as shown particularly by successful Japanese companies.

The Cecchini Report works upwards from a microeconomic to a macroeconomic level to show significant macroeconomic gains on all four economic objectives. Starting from a reduced rate of inflation, it shows that the difficult trade-off with unemployment can be much improved. Not only are new jobs created, but if governments or the EU so wish, there is leeway for additional aggregate economic reflation to create even more jobs. In addition, because of the valuable competitive supply-side improvements, then neither the public sector deficits nor the balance-of-payments position *vis-à-vis* the rest of the world need be jeopardized by economic expansion.

Overall, the Cecchini Report presented a very persuasive case for the SEM. Potentially it is a variable sum situation where all participants can derive potential benefits. Nevertheless, its success hinges on a progressive series of interlocking and reinforcing developments. These are underpinned by a boost in business expectations brought about by the permanent availability of a large market. Investment is boosted since businesses fear losing out to competitors who have invested aggressively in new plant and equipment. In reality, the early 1990s have been a period when many companies, especially small- and medium-sized enterprises (SMEs), have struggled in the recession, lacking sufficient resources to sustain themselves. Even larger companies have found that a standard market is only being developed slowly, often necessitating for the moment the continuing need for subtle and different national advertising campaigns. Furthermore, in the process of readjustment in the short run, more jobs are being lost before the beneficial medium-term projections of the SEM are reached.

Above all, though, the SEM neglected the regional implications of the policies proposed, since these are even more difficult to estimate.

Nevertheless, it seems likely that those countries which are strong in the service sector and high-tech industries, and which tend to be located more in the metropolitan and technopole regions, will benefit most. Although comparative advantage can change over time, those which already dominate the stronger industrial sector currently seem likely to do best. For example, Germany in particular is dominant in strong sectors and has relatively few weak sectors (Vickerman, 1992, p. 154). Another group of countries which comprises France, Belgium, the Netherlands, Italy and Ireland also tends to dominate stronger sectors. Given the regional problems in the latter two countries, this is promising news for them, though northern Italy is better placed to take advantage of the SEM than the Mezzogiorno.

Other weaker economies with major regional imbalance have been classified as having dominance in weaker industrial sectors; for example, the UK and Spain. However, a caveat to the analysis is that it is based only on industrial sectors, neglecting the strength of the UK economy in the service sector where opportunities exist and can be exploited more in the SEM. Finally, in Greece and Portugal, the two countries with the lowest living standards and major spatial inequalities, prospects look poor since they possess a large share of industrial employment in the weaker industrial sectors.

The weaker countries, particularly those in southern Europe, feel that despite the opportunities it presents, the SEM poses a major threat to them because of their lack of competitiveness and efficiencies in infrastructure. For example, all Spanish regions have expressed concern about weaknesses in their road and rail networks, insufficient technical innovation, lack of labour force skills, and so on (Leonardi (ed.), 1993, p. 209). Perhaps Catalonia is best placed, having more dynamic SMEs and a larger tertiary sector.

If countries in southern Europe engage in further inter-industry specialization in labour-intensive sectors where their strength lies, the likelihood in the long term is that they will still be overcome competitively by the newly industrializing countries (NICs). It is the latter which have the greatest comparative advantage in these labour-intensive sectors. Although Italian methods of adaptation by SMEs through subcontracting in sectors such as woollen textiles have shown that decline is not inevitable, ultimately the EU's advantage in the long run is unlikely to lie in labour-intensive production. A more appropriate strategy is probably one based on intra-industry specialization, often involving multinational companies. The latter, though, can create its own vulnerability unless it is accompanied by sufficient indigenous linkages.

It was recognized, therefore, that as a *quid pro quo* for the creation of the SEM and a business Europe, there would be a need to reinforce the role and expenditure of the structural funds. Otherwise those countries, particularly the ones in southern Europe, would have found it difficult to subscribe to further market integration without parallel redistributive regional and social measures.

EMU

The Treaty of Rome was mainly concerned to establish a Common Market and to introduce microeconomic rather than macroeconomic integration. Only the rudimentary aspects of monetary integration were considered, with stabilization of exchange rates, help in the case of balance-of-payments difficulties and some co-ordination of national policies (Molle, 1990, p. 390). Also, when the EC was first established, it was able to rely on the successful Bretton Woods fixed exchange rate system, and European economies enjoyed good rates of economic growth and high employment. This can be looked back upon as a golden age characterized by a high degree of real convergence in per capita Gross Domestic Product (GDP), with nominal convergence internally in low costs and prices and externally in exchange rate stability. However, the breakdown of the fixed exchange rate system in the late 1960s, with devaluation of sterling and the French franc and revaluation of the Deutschmark, created problems.

In 1969 at the Hague Summit, there was agreement to create an EMU and a blueprint for this was drawn up by P. Werner. This laid down a stage-by-stage plan to achieve EMU by 1980 through narrowing exchange rate margins, integrating capital markets and finally establishing a common currency and a single Central Bank. In 1972 there was the formation of the European currency band, the so-called 'snake', pegging EC currencies with fluctuations of up to plus or minus 2.25 per cent between member currencies (apart from the lira, which was allowed wider margins). The currencies came under repeated pressure and the UK, Italy and France all left the system, so that by 1978 it was mainly a Deutschmark zone consisting of Germany, the Netherlands, Belgium, Luxembourg and Denmark (which re-joined) plus Norway. Also, Austria was an informal associate member. The root of the problem of establishing a successful EMU in the 1970s lay in discordant economic policies (partly resulting from different reactions to the oil price increases) and an international preference for floating exchange rates.

There was renewed momentum to create a European Monetary System (EMS) by Roy Jenkins, President of the EC Commission in 1977, who argued that this was necessary to counter inflationary pressures. He engaged in close liaison with Giscard d'Estaing and Helmut Schmidt, and these close Franco-German relationships proved crucial in setting up a new monetary system. Germany was worried about the unstable dollar and the adverse effects of a continued movement into the Deutschmark, raising its value and hitting German exports and business profits. For France, it presented an opportunity to return to the monetary system of the EC and to stiffen its own anti-inflationary resolve. This was also true of Italy which, along with Ireland, gained additional regional assistance in return for membership. The UK saw the EMS more as a means of solving west German rather than British economic problems. It did not join the exchange rate mechanism initially and in so doing broke up the existing sterling system of the British Isles with the Republic of Ireland. However, sterling did form part of the new European currency basket.

The EMS was relatively successful, with fewer exchange rate realignments by the late 1980s, and the UK finally decided that the time was ripe to join in 1990. Unfortunately, as in the case of its original entry into the EC, it joined too late to derive significant benefits. In 1992 there was political uncertainty related to ratifying the Maastricht Agreement by member states. Also, the resources needed for successful German re-unification drove up interest rates. Currency turmoil in September 1992 led to the collapse of the Exchange Rate Mechanism (ERM) with the UK leaving acrimoniously, blaming German economic policy and the reluctance of the Bundesbank to support sterling. The cataclysm led to other members widening the currency band to plus or minus 15 per cent, apart from Germany and the Netherlands. In the UK, support through intervention for sterling was too late and the government's will to continue raising interest rates to defend the pound was doubted by the currency speculators. This was because existing high rates of unemployment would have been increased further by continuing to raise interest rates, crucifying the real economy. The British government preferred to float sterling rather than be seen to lose face by agreeing to devalue within the system, especially when unaccompanied by the willingness of strong countries to revalue.

Countries participating in the EMU have to modify their national macroeconomic preferences, reaching either some common preference or following the preference of the dominant economy, such as Germany. The consequence of weaker economies in trying to attain a lower rate of inflation is a much higher level of unemployment. However, given the monetarist perspective that no long-run trade-off exists between unemployment and inflation, countries were prepared to converge towards the lower German level of inflation. Unfortunately, the short-term consequence of this was heavy unemployment for weaker economies, leading to demands for even more structural funding for the areas worst affected. In addition, pressure is placed on politicians who are reluctant, given their short-term electoral horizons, to persevere with continued deflation when they can resort more readily to other measures.

Unfortunately, the EMU has tended to be operated in a deflationary way by Germany. Not only did this contribute to high unemployment, but further de-industrialization of some economies, for example, in Italy, although this was partly spared the magnitude of British de-industrialization by its large state sector and vibrant SMEs. The fixing of exchange rates in the short run provides some stability, but in the long run leads to a loss of flexibility. The final transition from fixity of exchange rates to a single currency would result in sacrificing this crucial instrument of economic policy. This element is amplified further in the next section examining the Maastricht Treaty and in particular the convergence criteria for an EMU.

THE MAASTRICHT TREATY

Negotiations were first launched in 1990 and concluded at Maastricht in the Netherlands in December 1991. The Treaty brings together the conclusions of the two intergovernmental conferences, one on political union and the other on monetary union. The Treaty on European Union combines the two texts in its 61,350 words and goes further than any other EC agreement in its aim of greater integration.

The Treaty is divided into seven Titles. Title 1 – Common Provisions – describes the Treaty as, 'a new stage in the process of creating an ever closer union among the peoples of Europe'. Title 2 is the largest section, dealing with Provisions amending the Treaty which established the EEC and including in particular EMU. Whilst the numbers of some of the major Articles in the original Treaty have been preserved, for example, numbers 85 and 86 relating to competition policy, others have been changed. Title 3 is 'Provisions amending the Treaty establishing the ECSC' (European Coal and Steel Community). Title 4 is 'Provisions amending the Treaty establishing the European Atomic Energy Community'. Title 5 is 'Provisions on a Common, Foreign and Security Policy'. This is a new pillar of the Community in addition to Title 6, which is 'Provisions on Co-operation in the fields of Justice and Home Affairs'. Title 7 is 'Final Provisions on Amendment to the Treaty and Accession by New Member States'. Following these seven Titles, there are 17 Protocols and 33 Declarations attached to the Final Act. The two Protocols which are most important to the UK relate to its exemptions to Stage 3 of EMU and to social policy which allows the other 11 countries to adopt a separate procedure.

Maastricht moves the European Economic Community to a European Community encompassing economic, political, social and cultural features. It also creates citizenship of the Union and this status brings forward a bundle of rights which include the right to move and reside freely in any member state and to vote and stand as a candidate in municipal elections, regardless of nationality. Any resident will also have the right to stand as a member of the European Parliament (EP) in the country of residence, regardless of birthplace or nationality. Another right is to receive diplomatic help from any member state which helps small countries, such as Luxembourg, in their dealings outside the EC. There is also Article 3b which established the principle of subsidiarity as a general principle: the Community takes action if it cannot be achieved better at national level.

There are many new areas of EC competence, including those relating to education; for example, encouraging language teaching, mobility and links between students and staff; and the mutual recognition of diplomas, certificates and other formal qualifications. Another new area is public health for research into, and prevention of, diseases. Knowledge of European culture, history and heritage is also to be improved.

Institutional changes which affect the EP include the latter's increased powers of amendment and greater conciliation with the European Council, and ultimately the possibility of a final veto by the EP. The EP will also have a greater role in appointing the EC Commission. Governments nominate Commissioners (in consultation with the EC President), but these need the assent of the EP which could reject the Commissioners. The EP's assent is also needed to major international agreements.

A new pillar is the beginnings of a common foreign and security policy through the Western European Union (WEU) (which could eventually include a common defence policy). It will be pursued in two ways: systematic co-operation (which already occurs within the framework of European political co-operation); and by common action within broad guidelines laid down by the European Council acting unanimously.

Another new pillar is intergovernmental co-operation on justice and home affairs. For example, asylum and immigration policy affecting third country nationals; also, co-operation in police matters, such as drugs and frauds. These two new policy areas have shifted from national control to Community control with power concentrated especially in the Council of Ministers (rather than the Commission). The EC is now at the centre of more affairs and these two new pillars were previously ones in which co-ordination was being carried out outside the EC framework.

There has also been reinforcement of economic and social cohesion with a new consultative Committee of the Regions and a new Cohesion Fund to help the four weakest member states: Spain, Greece, Portugal and Ireland. The Committee of the Regions has been promoted particularly by the German *Länder*. The latter have participated as representatives in the Council of Ministers with German ministers being accompanied by *Länder* ministers on regional matters and in other spheres where the *Länder* hold primary competence. Article 146 now says that the Council can be composed of representatives at ministerial level and no longer just government ministers. In addition to German pressure for stronger regional input, this has been reinforced by the growing decentralization in Belgium and to a lesser extent in Spain. It enshrines the subsidiarity principle of Maastricht. Like the Economic and Social Committee (ECOSOC), the new Committee has to be consulted on all matters of regional interest and to give its own opinions. Under Article 198c it is to be consulted where the Treaty lays down, namely structural funds, culture, public health, economic and social cohesion, and trans-European networks (TENs). Unfortunately, ECOSOC never developed a major role, especially after the enhanced powers given to the EP. Also, the procedure for appointment to the new Committee of the Regions by the Council on the recommendations of the member state's government tends to undermine its independence and power.

However, the new Committee of the Regions gives the regions recognition which they have lacked, apart from the creation in 1988 of the

Assembly of Regions and Local Authorities as an advisory body within DG XVI. The new Committee of the Regions enables the Commission to obtain other views than those of national governments, giving a real voice to local and regional government. It also represents a new approach, being 'bottom up' instead of 'top down'. The Committee will not only be consulted but may submit its own opinion on a matter where it believes that specific regional interests are involved. The Committee consists of 222 members, ranging from 24 for the large member states to an over-generous six for Luxembourg. The UK is atypical in lacking a formal tier of regional government and its membership of the Committee is drawn from elected local government representatives. By contrast, it is drawn from regional representatives in France, whilst in Belgium all the seats have been allocated to the regional councils. Divisions exist between the local representatives and the regionalists, with the latter from Belgium, Germany and Spain having a strong agenda for devolution. The Committee of the Regions is constrained in other ways since its opinions may be rejected by the Council or Commission; also it is unable to deliver its opinions to the European Parliament and cannot bring legal actions to the European Court of Justice. Notwithstanding its limitations this new body representing subnational interests is a useful democratic addition to the institutional framework.

The regions will also be helped by the Cohesion Fund to finance projects in fields of environment and transport infrastructure. In addition, the Community has taken a new policy initiative on TENs in transport, telecommunications and energy infrastructures. Support can be given to national programmes, particularly through feasibility studies, loan guarantees or interest subsidies, as well as through the Cohesion Fund for transport infrastructure.

In relation to the UK, the opt-out on social policy and EMU is a pointer to the future in framing a more variable geometry Europe and this will be helpful in relation to new members of the EU in the near future. The social agreement led to 11 member states concluding an agreement for implementation of the 1989 Social Charter (from which the UK excluded itself). The 11 have agreed that the following issues can be decided by qualified majority vote: health and safety; working conditions; information and consultation of workers; equality at work between men and women; and integration of persons excluded from the labour market. Issues for unanimous vote cover: social security and social protection of workers; protection of workers made redundant; representation and collective defence of workers and employers; conditions of employment for third country nations; and financial contributions for promoting jobs.

EMU AND MAASTRICHT

In the past, the promotion of monetary union as a precondition for forcing economic union was 'putting the cart before the horse'. Only with economic convergence via economic union is a durable EMU feasible. This economic perspective is recognized mainly in the Maastricht Agreement. But Stage 1 was launched under existing EC powers from 1 July 1990, with action taken to improve economic and monetary co-ordination between member states, and to extend the work of the Committee of Central Bank Governors. Stages 2 and 3 necessitate changes in the Treaty since they involve setting up new institutions. These involve in Stage 2 from 1 January 1994 the establishment of a European Monetary Institute to strengthen co-operation between national central banks and to co-ordinate monetary policies.

Four convergence criteria have been established in order to pass to Stage 3 of EMU. Inflation is not to be more than 1.5 per cent above that of the best three performing states. In 1992 these were Belgium, Denmark and France, whose rates ranged from 2.1 per cent to 2.8 per cent, hence the reference value for inflation ranged from 3.6 per cent to 4.3 per cent. Five other member states satisfied this criterion, the exceptions being Greece, Portugal, Italy and Spain. An additional convergence criterion is that long-term interest rates are to be within 2 per cent of the three lowest member states. This again is to keep a watchful long-term eye on inflationary expectations. At the end of 1993 eight out of 12 countries were meeting the interest rate and inflation criteria. The collapse of the normal exchange rate bands of plus or minus 2.25 per cent has thrown the exchange rate criterion into disarray. The normal fluctuation margins of the ERM should have been respected for two years without severe tensions and without a devaluation on a member state's own initiative. However, with the severe tensions since September 1992, are we to take the bands as plus or minus 2.25 per cent, or plus or minus 15 per cent? Also, is devaluation on one's own initiative to be excluded where realignments have been mutually agreed as they usually are in the system? The UK, Italy and Greece are not in the ERM. However, France has succeeded in getting the franc back to narrow margins; and as a result of the exchange rate realignments, the stage may be set for greater exchange rate durability in the immediate future.

A fourth criterion involves greater prudence to meet the new Maastricht budgetary limits. The ratio of planned or actual government deficit to GDP is not to exceed 3 per cent, though the Commission may be tolerant provided the ratio has declined and is close to this, or alternatively if it is just over 3 per cent, but this is exceptional and temporary. Another condition is that the ratio of government debt to GDP is not to exceed 60 per cent, though again the Commission may be tolerant providing that the ratio is dropping sufficiently and approaching the 60 per cent limit at a satisfactory pace (Wildavsky and Zapico-Goni (eds), 1993, p. 74). In 1992 there were only four EC countries (Denmark, France, Ireland and Luxembourg) which had a budgetary deficit below 3 per cent, though Germany and the Netherlands could be considered borderline. Also in 1992 only five member states (Germany, Spain, France, Luxembourg and the UK) had a gross debt to GDP ratio of less than 60 per cent. The growing recession and high unemployment have worsened the situation, so on a strict interpretation only France and Luxembourg were achieving the joint criteria. Therefore much hinges on economic recovery and the continued degree of commitment of member states to accepting a further tightening of their national budgetary situations. For example, the UK, despite its Medium-Term Financial Strategy committing it to balancing the budget over the medium term, moved from a short-lived budgetary surplus to a large budgetary deficit of about 8 per cent of GDP, which necessitated significant and unpopular tax increases by the Chancellor Kenneth Clarke in 1993–94. Whilst the Maastricht budgetary conditions do not impose automatic national expenditure cuts, with some leniency in times of slump, they do narrow even further the room for national manoeuvre and contra-cyclical stabilization policies.

Stage 2 of EMU runs to 1 January 1997 if convergence criteria are met by a majority of member states (which is seven out of 12, or six if the UK does not take part in Stage 3). Without a majority, the fall-back date for EMU to begin irrevocably is 1 January 1999. We will then have in Stage 3 a European Central Bank (ECB) with a central monetary policy. All national bank governors are part of the ECB, plus some independent members. The Bank's aim is to pursue price stability. It is based in Frankfurt, giving some reward to Germany for giving up the Deutschmark for the European Currency Unit (ECU). As national central banks become more independent of government, only with reluctance will they surrender some of their new found powers to the ECB. Furthermore, the UK and Denmark have an opt-out from Stage 3 of the Maastricht Agreement. If the UK does not join Stage 3, it retains all its powers for monetary and exchange rate policy and will not be subject to EU disciplines, apart from its commitment not to run excessive budgetary deficits. The UK would also have no right to participate in the appointment of officers to the executive of the ECB and its statutes would not apply in the UK. Thus the likelihood is that EMU will only go ahead with a smaller number of countries than the original 12, perhaps with a delayed timetable.

WIDENING OF THE EU

This section looks at the enlargement of the EU both in the past and into the future. It was the widening from six member states initially to nine member states in 1973 which increased regional inequalities. Until that time, apart from southern Italy, the EC had enjoyed fairly balanced development and relatively full employment. After 1973 this changed, with the oil crisis creating stagflation. Also, the northern enlargement added regional problems in the most peripheral states, particularly Ireland.

During the 1980s southern enlargement aggravated the national, regional and social imbalance even further. Greece was incorporated fully into the EC after its long Association Agreement. Spain joined, after its relative isolation under Franco, whilst Portugal followed the switch of other countries away from EFTA. Membership was a reward to southern Europe for its retreat from dictatorship to democracy.

The enlargement process has resumed in the 1990s, with Austria, Sweden, Finland and Norway having been offered membership of the EU, with acceptance being dependent on national referenda. Positive ratification has occurred for the first three countries, but this was taken too much for granted, as on a previous occasion in 1972, in the case of Norwegian rejection. Norway had centuries of isolation, first as a colony of Denmark, then of Sweden. It now values its independence and is worried about loss of sovereignty. In economic terms it is wealthy, with natural resources: forestry, fisheries and energy, such as hydroelectric power, and oil (with its production greatly exceeding its domestic consumption), resulting in a significant export surplus. In the EU it would have been peripheral, with opposition especially in the more northerly underpopulated regions.

The countries in EFTA already have very close trading links with the EU and wish to benefit further from full SEM membership. Also, political constraints for them have lessened with the demise of the threatening political and military power of the USSR. As richer countries they will be net contributors to the EU budget. Whilst Sweden and Finland have marked regional problems in the more northerly parts of their territories, and in agriculture will have to adjust to lower EU prices, overall their entry into the EU is free of major problems and seems sensible. Only Norway and Switzerland have continuing reservations to impede their full membership of the EU.

Further Mediterranean enlargement to include Malta and Cyprus seems unlikely to cause major difficulties since these islands are small. The EU already has countries with much lower incomes per head and wider regional problems. Cyprus has an income per head higher than that of Greece or Portugal. It is keen to move on from its customs union to full membership, partly to benefit in the SEM from its large service sector. It has been meeting the Maastricht convergence conditions and has pegged its currency to the EMU. Malta lacks the entrepreneurial flair of the Cypriot business community and its very small firms face more painful readjustment. However, Malta stands to benefit significantly from budgetary transfers, despite its very small agricultural sector, of roughly three times more than its contributions (Redmond, 1993, pp. 122–3). The Maltese shipyards would also be eligible for EU RENAVAL expenditure subsidies.

The political problems relating to both Cyprus and Malta have constituted a more significant constraint; for example, with Turkey's continued occupation of the northern part of Cyprus. Meanwhile, in Malta, party political differences have existed between the more pro-EU Nationalist Party and the historically anti-EU Labour Party. Malta's preference has been for neutrality and non-participation in a common foreign, security and defence arrangement.

The greatest problems of enlargement are in dealing with the other countries in eastern Europe knocking on the door of the EU for full membership, plus Turkey. Nevertheless, the EU is under pressure to offer more, since the Europe Agreements with eastern Europe, though helpful, are seen by the latter to be overly restrictive in limiting their full growth potential. The EU has also had considerable resort to antidumping and safeguard measures against what it considers to be unfair imports. Yet even with faster economic development in eastern Europe, the range of regional inequalities will be enormous, ranging from the new Scandinavian enlargement in northern Europe to the countries of southern Europe, eastern Europe and Turkey. Within eastern Europe alone there is a wide variation from the most prosperous, the Czech Republic, to the poorest, Romania.

If the model of EU integration is that of the USA, then it might be argued that the EU can easily absorb all of these European states in its membership. The EU derives increased power and prestige from its continued growth and size. In addition, the marginal costs of some of its activities fall when new members are added and share the same overhead costs of operating the organization. Unfortunately, however, some costs rise if completely new institutional capacity has to be created to cater for new members, plus all the additional costs of language, interpretation and translation. Furthermore, the marginal benefit to the EU from adding new countries inevitably diminishes, more so when they have low income per head. The accommodation of countries with a low level of economic development, involving high dependence on agriculture and marked regional imbalance, will create enhanced cost pressures and be a source of tension. Countries such as Germany will prove reluctant paymasters since they have had to spend vast sums to improve the position in the eastern *Länder*. Despite the citizenship status in the Maastricht Agreement, the focus may be more on German citizenship than on European citizenship if the latter involves continuing high levels of regional aid to a growing number of recipients in southern and eastern Europe. Also, the poorer countries of southern Europe may fear a displacement of the benefits and assistance which they currently enjoy to even poorer newcomers in eastern Europe.

It may be argued that the EU is in a classic catch 22 situation in which further enlargement is costly, but non-enlargement is even more costly if eastern Europe dissolves into economic chaos. Such instability may lead to the resumption of a costly arms race. The EU already provides significant aid to eastern Europe, though the budgetary costs of full membership may be higher. For example, enlargement to include the Visegrad 4 (Hungary, Czech and Slovak republics, Poland) plus the Balkan and Baltic republics would require an additional 0.85 per cent of EC GDP by 1999. If the republics of the former USSR were included it would rise by a further 1.3 per cent of EC GDP: this is an amount similar to the existing budget currently for the whole of the EC (12) (*European Economy*, 1993, p. 114). However, in trade with eastern

Europe the EU is projected to have an overall trade surplus. According to a Commission Report – 'Trade and Foreign Investment in the Community Regions: The Impact of Economic Reform in Eastern Europe', (CEC, 1993a) – it is shown that there is also sufficient foreign investment around to flow to eastern Europe and not be wholly diverted to southern Europe. Eastern Europe is perceived to have no significant advantage, such as skill levels (CEC, 1993a, p. 13). This may be questionable, given the author's experience of the educational levels in countries such as Hungary and Poland, and also where wage costs are really very low in relation to the potential for productivity increases.

Overall, the EU needs to be discerning in deciding where to draw the line on future enlargement; for example, probably excluding nearly all the Commonwealth of Independent States (of the former Soviet Union) (CIS) and Turkey. For those countries which are to join, a long time-horizon will be necessary. A first useful stage would be for many of the applicants to co-operate together initially to promote their mutual trade links, as exemplified by the Visegrad Group. As more advanced countries vacate EFTA en route to the EU, EFTA might provide a useful starting point for some of these countries. Finally, when they join the EU, after completing the transition to political democracy and market economies, the EU is likely to insist on a long period for adaptation and adjustment for new members. Setting a clear date for membership would be helpful, perhaps the year 2000, and also clear criteria; for instance, satisfying the Maastricht conditions, plus others relating to the increasing size of the private sector. Though eastern European countries have made great strides, their main macroeconomic failing is still caused by high rates of inflation, necessitating currency devaluation, as in the 'crawling peg' depreciation of the Polish zloty.

Enlargement always involves a two-way adjustment and the EU itself will have to restructure some of its own economic sectors. For example, in agriculture there will be increased imports from eastern Europe. Fortunately, the welfare effect on the EU will be limited since consumers will benefit from lower prices. Several manufacturing industries, such as steel, will be badly hit and greater funding will be necessary by Resider (see Chapter 5). Meanwhile, eastern Europe itself will require massive amounts of aid for its own regions, especially in the more backward and easterly regions. Whilst some city areas are close to full employment, such as the Czech capital Prague and cities in the western parts of other countries, such as Poznan in Poland, the more remote agricultural areas in the east would absorb a massive amount of funding to modernize and develop their local economies. Their problems have been aggravated by the collapse in trade with the CIS and reorientation in the pattern of trade towards the EU. Infrastructure improvements are crucial, for example, to railways where there is often much single track, as in Hungary. The likelihood is that links to the EU, whilst benefiting the more western regions, will not help the more remote eastern regions sufficiently.

2. Trends in employment: the lack of jobs

JOB CREATION

The EC was much less successful than its competitors in creating new jobs between 1970 and 1990. Whereas the US created 30 million jobs over 20 years without out-performing the EU in terms of the pace of economic growth, the EU created only 10 million: these were mainly for women, with the number of men in employment falling slightly.

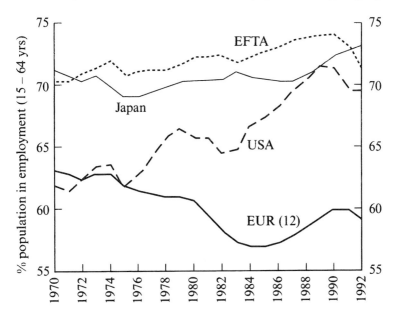

Source: CEC (1993e).

Figure 2.1   Employment rates in the Community and elsewhere, 1970–92

This is shown in Figure 2.1 and indicates that the share of the EC working age population in employment was lower in 1992 than 20 years earlier.

Despite some significant improvement in job creation during 1985–90, on average 1.5 per cent per annum, for the previous 15 years the EC's record had been poor. Only in the late 1980s did its improvement come close to the impressive performance of the USA and Japan, where employment in 1990 had risen to 72–75 per cent of the working age population (CEC, 1991a, p. 21). Since then the EU has been affected again by recession and there are continuing worries about its weak trade performance. The EU's main trade strength is naturally in the European market itself, plus Africa, the Middle East and eastern Europe. Unfortunately it accounts for less than 25 per cent of US imports of manufactured goods, and under 15 per cent in Asia where markets are expanding most rapidly.

Whilst the EU and the USA are both affected by structural change, the former has been less successful in generating new employment opportunities. One explanation lies in the more welfare-concentrated European system of social security and health benefits. In the USA, by comparison, workers after six months lose unemployment benefits, and with unemployment comes the loss of free and generous company health benefits. In the USA workers face pressure to take low paid jobs. Hence the EU maintains a benefit system and a floor to incomes but at the cost of higher levels of unemployment. In the EU unemployment remains stuck at high levels, whereas in the USA it has fallen back to earlier and lower levels. In terms of inequalities an important issue is the degree to which one is prepared to see economic and social divisions within developed countries which at the bottom reflect those of Third World economies.

A higher rate of economic growth is obviously conducive to the growth of employment opportunities. Apart from this employment intensity, an employment threshold is the percentage change above which the growth rate of GDP results in an increase in employment. In fact, this employment threshold has been higher than in the 1960s and fairly stable over the last 15–20 years. This undermines those who adhere to a thesis of economic growth without jobs. The employment threshold corresponds by definition to the trend of apparent labour productivity in the economy (CEC, 1994d, p. 57).

The rate of growth of Community GDP has fallen steadily compared with the period 1960–73. In that period EC GDP grew at 4.8 per cent per annum. A lower rate of job creation matched the low increase in labour supply of 0.3 per annum on average. This kept unemployment low, at an average of 2.6 per cent per annum during 1960–73. Between 1974 and 1985, after the oil price crisis, the rate of economic growth in the EC dropped to an average of 2 per cent per annum. The labour force also increased by 0.7 per cent per annum on average. Even though employment intensity increased slightly, by 1985 unemployment had risen to 10.8 per cent. The recovery in economic growth from 1986–90 was particularly welcome and it averaged 3.2 per cent per annum. Employment intensity remained high, and unemployment dropped back to 8.3 per cent in 1990. During the 1990s the rate of economic growth has slowed down again and in 1993 it actually became negative for the first time since 1975.

The US rate of economic growth during 1970–92, though slightly less than that in the EC, was far more successful in job creation. The US rate of economic growth during 1973–90 averaged 2.3 per cent per annum, and with labour productivity rising only slowly at 0.4 per cent per annum (with real wages also rising by 0.4 per cent per annum) the average rate of increase of employment was 1.9 per cent per annum. Despite a fall in the rate of growth of US GDP during 1990–92, this did not result in a major fall in its employment level.

The target set by the EU Commission for the creation of at least 15 million new jobs by the year 2000 through a 2 per cent per annum increase in employment is desirable but seems unlikely to be attained. For example, between 1984 and 1990 the EC created just over 9 million net new jobs. However, up to the year 2000 EU labour supply is forecast to rise by about 0.5 per cent per annum (comprising an increased participation rate of 0.7 per cent per annum and an increased population of working age of 0.5 per cent per annum). Therefore, just to cater for this increase in labour supply and keep unemployment stable it will be necessary to create 5 million new jobs. The EU is much in need of either a better rate of economic growth and/or an improved record of employment creation. It is unable to match the example of Japan in terms of the pace of economic growth, high productivity and employment creation (though the latter is lower in Japan than in the USA). The EU is torn between adopting Japanese-style methods to increase productivity and American labour-intensive methods of employment growth in low paid occupations. However, even with high growth, such as that of the Spanish economy during 1970–92 when economic growth was better than that of the US, Spain's employment record has been appalling with a complete inability to create new jobs in aggregate. The link between economic growth and job creation varies significantly. For example, in 1985–90 EC economic growth averaged 3 per cent per annum, but net job creation was just over 1 per cent per annum.

The degree of job creation is determined by the extent to which productivity rises, and this was lower in most EC countries during 1985–90 than previously. The slowdown in productivity is attributable largely to many low productivity jobs with insufficient investment. Also, it may be related partly to the switch towards a larger service sector. In all member states more than 50 per cent of civilian employment is now in services, ranging from just over 50 per cent in Greece to 70 per cent in the Netherlands. This is shown in Figure 2.2.

However, growing employment in the service sector alone is not the most persuasive explanation since, according to the Commission, output per person is similar in services to that in industry (CEC 1991a, p. 28). The slowdown in productivity growth may be explained better

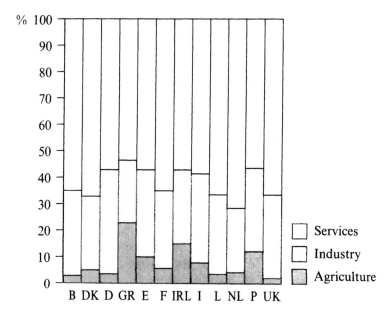

Source: *Eurostat*, Luxembourg: OOPEC, 1993.

Figure 2.2   Distribution of civilian employment in agriculture, industry and services

by recognizing that using the number of persons employed conceals the fact that employees work shorter hours these days and more of them work on a part-time basis. However, even after taking this into account it still shows little change to productivity levels (apart from in the Netherlands where there is a high part-time workforce). In the Netherlands in 1991 average weekly hours worked were 33 hours per week and in Denmark 35 hours per week.

Despite the EU's optimistic improvement in job creation during 1985–90, the EU economy fell into macroeconomic difficulties in the early 1990s. Insufficient new jobs have been created to keep pace with the rapid growth of the labour force, especially in southern European countries. Furthermore, whilst jobs are obviously welcome, there is not an equivalent reduction made to rates of unemployment. This is because only about a third of the jobs are taken by people officially registered as unemployed and the rest are filled by young people entering the labour force for the first time and by those joining the labour force from inactivity. More is said about the latter and the growing importance of female employment in Chapter 6.

UNEMPLOYMENT

The rate of unemployment in the EU has risen significantly since 1970 and remains far above that in the USA and Japan. This is illustrated graphically (Figure 2.3) over the ten year period 1983–92, showing the much higher total unemployment in the EU and also the higher unemployment for both males and females. In Germany, for example, in the Federal Republic in 1992 unemployment stood at 6.6 per cent but in the eastern *Länder*, including east Berlin, unemployment was 14.8 per cent. Also, unlike the Federal Republic, female unemployment in the eastern *Länder* was greatly in excess of male unemployment. These unemployment statistics exclude short-time workers, along with those on job creation schemes and those who were able to take early retirement. The direct economic costs of unemployment, including the payment of social security benefits plus the loss of direct tax which would be paid, was put at over ECU 200 billion for the EU in 1993, which is similar to the whole of GDP in Belgium. These costs are also an underestimate in excluding the lower indirect taxes collected in addition to all the other social costs of unemployment. Costs of unemployment are shown in Figure 2.4 for each member state.

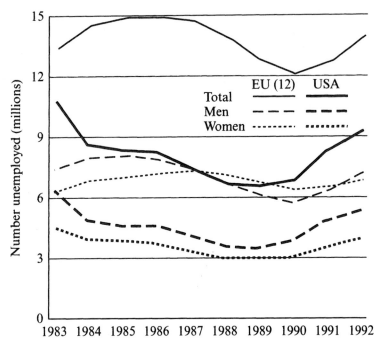

Source: *Eurostat*, Luxembourg: OOPEC, 1994.

*Figure 2.3   Evolution of unemployment levels, EU (12) and USA,
1983–92*

Even with fairly optimistic predictions of economic growth averaging 3 per cent per annum, the unemployment rate in the EU is unlikely to fall back below 10 per cent in the next few years. Workers feel insecure compared with those in other countries such as Japan, where more than a third of workers have lifetime employment up to the age of 55, after which they receive a bonus for a few more years or are found another job. The large Japanese companies in particular offer a job for life, with employees committed to work flexibly in return for all the welfare benefits provided by the company. Married women and employees in the smaller firms are treated far more as the variable elements in the labour market.

The labour market consists of the following elements: the employed labour force and the unemployed job seekers, who together comprise the active working population; finally there is the inactive population of

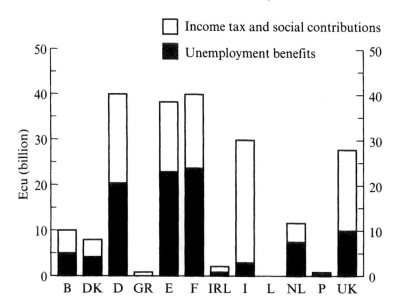

Source: CEC (1994d), p. 141.

Figure 2.4   The cost of unemployment in the member states, 1993

working age. The pool of unemployment rises when it cannot absorb the large number of new entrants into the labour market, such as school leavers and re-entrants such as married women. Workers are being laid off, fired or made redundant, whilst others voluntarily quit their jobs and search for new employment. Unemployment increases if these inflows into the labour market are in excess of outflows into jobs, or into retirement, full-time education, or non-market work (as in the home). There is a continuous movement of people between jobs, but unemployment does not affect everyone to the same degree; for example, it tends to possess a U-shape as age increases, with high unemployment for young people just entering the labour market and again for older workers. There is also increasing concern about long-term unemployment. The concept of hysteresis argues that unemployment causes more unemployment since employers decide that the unemployed have lost the work habit and their skills have become rusty. Meanwhile the unemployed get discouraged, lose work contacts and start to accept their unemployment predicament, giving up their search for work.

There are three main perspectives on unemployment: technical change, the level of aggregate demand and, finally, supply-side factors.

Technical Change

Technical change is creating rapid microeconomic displacement of workers, with 10–15 per cent of jobs being destroyed each year. However, at the macroeconomic level it can also create new jobs: Japan, for instance, has the lowest rate of unemployment. Technical changes increase productivity, lower prices and raise demand. However, the scale of new technology, especially when concerned more with process than product innovation, is displacing workers, increasingly replacing them by robotics in many industries such as car assembly. Unfortunately there is little choice about deferring the application of new technology, since competitors who introduce it are able to steal a competitive edge. Countries which were partly insulated from the latest technology, such as those in the eastern European Council for Mutual Economic Assistance (COMECON) bloc, maintained low unemployment until their system eventually collapsed. The process of technical change is wreaking havoc on those without new skills. Whilst demand for skilled workers is rising, the unskilled are seeing their jobs exported abroad by multinational companies. European labour-intensive industries are being de-industrialized. Workers are being displaced either into the service sector (and often into part-time jobs filled mainly by women) or directly into the growing dole queues. The role of technical change is taken up again in explaining long waves in a later section in this chapter.

Level of Aggregate Demand

Problems in the EU which arise from the side of demand can be measured not just from unemployment statistics, but also require the use of vacancy statistics. However, the latter tend to be less reliable since many firms with vacancies advertise them but do not record them with the official employment authorities. Therefore, the vacancy statistics need adjusting upwards and once this has been done they can be taken to reflect the amount of frictional and structural unemployment. Frictional unemployment is relatively unimportant and can be reduced by increased provision of information. Improving the operation of the labour market by increased occupational and geographical mobility will also help to reduce structural unemployment. However, since unemployment (*U*) has been well in excess of vacancies (*V*) for many years, then *U* – *V* measures the level of demand-deficient unemployment.

Keynesian analysis has favoured raising the aggregate level of demand (consumption + investment + government expenditure + exports – imports). Keynes elevated the importance of government expenditure to fill the gap left by a deficient expenditure by the private sector. A high level of aggregate demand has had great success in reducing aggregate unemployment, particularly during the 1950s and 1960s. Unfortunately it has subsequently run into other problems of inflation, balance-of-payments deficits and budgetary deficits tending to crowd out the private sector. Whereas in Keynes's analysis government expenditure led to multiplier effects crowding in the private sector (though he did not use the word 'crowding'), in recent years critics have focused on its displacement effects in crowding out the private sector. This rests on the critical assumption that the private sector will invest and neglects the importance of Keynes's assertion that the essence of the unemployment problem lies in the uncertainty and lack of complete information which prevents and dampens private sector intentions.

Frequently during the 1980s countries in the EU tended to adopt deflationary fiscal policies to tackle their newly perceived problems, invariably accompanied by tight monetary policies. The latter were followed particularly by the weaker countries adhering to fixed exchange rates within the EMS. These high interest rates crippled private sector investment. Only with the collapse of the EMS fixed exchange rates and more realistic market rates have interest rates fallen, pulling countries such as the UK out of deep recession with a rapid economic recovery.

It is recognized that for sustained economic growth in the case of demand there is a chronic need to increase the level of investment. This takes the form of both widening and deepening of capital. The former adds more of the same capital whilst the latter results in more sophisticated technological methods of production. Investment, however, is determined far more by business expectations of being able to make a profit. Economic growth in the EU started to fall towards the end of 1990, mainly because of the collapse in business investment. Gross fixed capital formation, which had shown an annual real percentage change of 6.4 on average between 1986 and 1989, fell to zero in 1991 and showed only a 0.4 per cent increase in 1992 (CEC, 1994a, p. 5). Firms now need to recognize that with much lower rates of inflation they need not seek such high rates of return. The target, according to some commentators, should be zero short-term interest rates (CEC, 1994a, p. 87). Consumer expenditure during the early 1990s also contributed to weakening domestic demand, with inflation contributing to the sharp decline in real disposable income. Consumer expenditure, which had risen on average at 3.9 per cent per annum during 1986–89, fell to 1.4 per cent in 1992.

There is also a need to increase investment; for example, through public sector infrastructure and housing. However, rising public sector deficits conflict with the Maastricht convergence conditions. If these are to be adhered to, it will mean further inroads have to be made in some welfare expenditure, however undesirable the cuts may be on equity considerations. Whilst the Edinburgh Summit provided a stimulus to increasing investment in the EU in the 1990s, this will need to be on an even larger scale.

The changing composition of demand away from the public sector towards the private sector through privatization has also started to have significant consequences, and this is discussed later.

Supply-Side Factors

Supply-side factors are also important, with firms critical of excessively high wage rates because of trades union bargaining power and/or minimum wage intervention. Trades unions have developed historically to counter employer exploitation, with unions using various threats and sanctions, such as strike action. However, since labour time cannot be stored, unions prefer to reach a satisfactory collective wage bargaining settlement rather than an all-out strike, though uncertainty and lack of complete information about each side's real intentions does result in industrial action and inflationary wage settlements. The ideal situation from the viewpoint of running the economy closer to its employment potential is to keep wages more in line with productivity increases. Attempts to do this have varied, including more centralized collective bargaining with a government input to represent the national interest through use of prices and incomes policies. At the other extreme, more decentralized collective bargaining conducted in a responsible manner and with a weakened trades union representation has also been followed.

Although trades unions might be desirable in monopsony conditions to create countervailing power, the more prevalent competitive market conditions mean that higher wages result in increased unemployment and have inflationary consequences. The increase in unemployment is higher where supply and demand for labour are both highly elastic. If firms cannot increase productivity to pay higher wages, they have to raise their prices. Minimum wages are also inflationary if those on higher incomes and with stronger bargaining power are also determined to maintain their wage differentials. The effects of minimum wage legislation clearly depend upon the level at which these are set and at a higher level only protect those fortunate enough to remain in employment, with even more adverse effects at higher levels on both unemployment and inflation. Attitudes to low pay and the respective roles of the state and trades unions in raising minimum pay have been shaped by national historical traditions. The UK has only ever had limited minimum wage legislation for particularly low paid trades, but the Conservative government since 1979 has intensified its onslaught on trades unions and Wage Councils which set minimum pay in a small number of low paid sectors. All of the Wage Councils have been swept away, apart from that in agriculture. The preference in the UK has generally been to tackle poverty through fiscal redistribution rather than directly distorting the labour market through universal minimum wages. This issue of intervention in the labour market and the contrasting view of the EU in wishing to develop a more extensive social policy is at variance with a free market preference by the Conservative government in the UK.

The main problem underlying unemployment in the EU is wage 'stickiness', compared with greater flexibility of wages in the USA (where trades unions are weaker) and also in Japan (assisted through the system of annual bonuses which fluctuate in response to the profitability of the enterprise). Where wages are more rigid, quantities have to adjust; that is, via more unemployment. Whereas in the neo-Keynesian model contract theory binds workers and employers together with stable real wages and employment variability, neoclassical analysis focuses more upon job search. Workers seek to maximize their lifetime earnings though they have less information about wages and unemployment as they move upwards from local labour markets to regional, inter-regional and international labour markets. They have to engage in a thorough search for the best job and they do this from the position of being out of work because of the time needed to be devoted to an intensive job search. For example, studies have shown the unemployed spending on average five hours per week on job search, with some people spending nearly 20 hours a week on this. The ability to search for the best employment hinges on the availability of benefits, with higher benefits increasing search duration. Unemployed workers receive unemployment benefits, welfare benefits and tax rebates which constitute their replacement ratio when not in work. Whilst it is necessary to compensate those unemployed who are the losers in the process of economic and technical change, the level of compensation should not be so high as to maintain a reservation wage below which jobs are not taken. Until job searchers revise their expectations downwards and scrap their outdated reservation wages, voluntary frictional unemployment will tend to persist at a high level.

Firms are reluctant to take on labour because of supply-side impediments created by trades unions and governmental intervention, another example of the latter being the extra social costs which are levied on employment. Unemployment is aggravated in a vicious circle of high taxes to finance a high level of governmental spending, with statutory charges around 40 per cent of EU GDP. Furthermore, costs of social contributions on labour are equivalent to 23.5 per cent of GDP (CEC, 1994d, p. 153). These labour charges on average in the EU are shared two-thirds by employers and one-third by employees, with some variation from country to country. Non-wage costs are much higher in France, Belgium and Italy than in the UK and Denmark. Often the higher non-wage costs tend to be offset by lower wage costs (since taxes are lower); but this means it just reflects the way the social welfare system is financed. Nevertheless, it has been argued that the level of these extra costs hits the most labour-intensive firms, particularly SMEs, and encourages the black economy. Econometric models show that reducing these statutory charges by 1 per cent of GDP would tend to reduce unemployment by 2.5 per cent over four years (CEC, 1994d, p. 156). Governments need to reduce the charges and raise more money from other sources, such as energy taxes, excise duties and value added tax. In the longer term EU labour charges need to be brought down closer to the levels which prevail in the USA or Japan.

Whilst labour costs vary, unit labour costs are more important in relation to productivity. On this basis labour is still relatively cheap in the Netherlands and Luxembourg (despite high wages there) and also fairly cheap in Portugal and Ireland. It is, however, relatively expensive in Germany and Denmark (CEC, 1993e, p. 13). There are also marked regional variations which are widest in Italy and narrowest in Germany, but even so labour costs in the Mezzogiorno in 1988 in manufacturing industry were still only 15 per cent lower than in northern Italy. The variation was larger between industries inter-regionally, such as clothing and footwear, where costs were roughly 40 per cent lower in southern Italy: a range of this magnitude is needed to stimulate regional development.

Wages do not fall sufficiently even when unemployment is high because 'outsiders' are not perceived by employers to have the requisite skills, and the outsiders themselves, especially the long-term unemployed, have allowed their skills to rust and have often given up searching for work. The phenomenon of hysteresis has occurred in which the longer people are unemployed, the more likely they are to remain unemployed. Employment policy therefore has to address in particular the problem of long-term unemployment and try to reduce the costs to employers. The 1994 UK budget measures included some imaginative proposals; for example, by providing a national insurance holiday to employers taking on those unemployed for over two years. The new arrangements for employers to hand over national insurance on a quarterly instead of a monthly basis will also reduce administrative costs, helping SMEs especially in job creation. The Conservative government has also cut back on the benefit system available to those out of work. Now more positive carrots are offered to the unemployed; for example, search costs are reduced through Community Action providing help in looking for work, whilst the Jobseekers' Allowance provides direct compensation for search costs. Further help is offered by exempting the Back to Work bonus from tax. A Jobfinders' Grant to the long-term unemployed who find work helps to cover other costs. Further help is given to ensure those taking up work will be better off than remaining unemployed on benefits.

The supply-side measures needed include better training and retraining which reduce unemployment in the short run, whilst new skills reduce unemployment in the long run (these are financed by the European Social Fund (ESF) and discussion is covered later in Chapter 6). Also, a continued reduction in working hours is important. The length of the basic working week has continued to fall during the 20th century and this will need to be accelerated. One could create in theory a Utopian society in which work was shared out for all and people chose their leisure, instead of millions experiencing forced leisure (and minimal income) as a result of unemployment. Generally the assumption is that in richer economies, as wages rise, workers will choose at the margin to substitute leisure for work. Working hours, defined as all hours worked including overtime and whether paid or not, have fallen over the last ten years in all member states apart from the UK. Working hours in the UK were 43.4 hours per week in 1992, which is one hour more than in 1983. It was also over two hours higher than in the country with the next highest working hours, Portugal, with 41 hours per week on average. Apart from Greece and Spain, other member states have broken through and gone below 40 hours per week, with Belgium being lowest at 38.2 hours per week. If the UK had continued its long-run trend to a shorter working week throughout the 1980s then up to an extra million jobs might have been created.

Apparent anomalies are the practices of significant overtime working and dual job-holding amidst high unemployment. Overtime working has been done by workers who felt unable to manage on their basic wage, and by employers who required extra output. However, employers, given business uncertainty and the costs of employing new workers (wages plus all the other social costs of employment), preferred to incur just the marginal wage cost of overtime for existing employees. They did not want to be faced with all the other costs of interviewing, recruiting, training and perhaps ultimately declaring redundant the new employees.

Dual job-holding is more open to criticism when a person has a full-time well-paid job plus another one, rather than the situation of a worker having two part-time jobs. The disadvantage of controlling working hours is the infringement of choice for employees, but control is advocated in the interests of those for whom there appears to be little choice but that of unemployment. Currently the number of hours worked per annum are 1 700 in the EU (with Germany being lowest at 1 550), compared with 1 800 per annum in the USA and 2 050 in Japan (Holland, 1993, p. 142). Clearly any legislation has to occur at the EU level, otherwise countries reducing working hours without either increasing productivity (for example, to German levels) or reducing pay proportionately would be uncompetitive. The EU is to phase in a highly qualified maximum of 48 working hours per week.

S. Holland (1993), idealizing the Japanese model, sees European workers, in return for a shorter number of hours and flexitime, delivering increased productivity and flexibility; for example, multi-skill training and regular retraining every few years. However, the point he misses is that the EU will still remain less competitive unless Japan also reduces its working hours, and the prospects for that are limited for a workaholic society and one with low unemployment.

PRIVATIZATION

Privatization is also beginning to impinge on the level of employment, and in the short term redundancies are being created to increase profitability. Pressures for privatization lie mainly at national level and the EU is largely indifferent about public/private ownership, though the latter is more consistent with facilitating competition policy. Also, other EU countries have followed the UK lead towards privatization. For example, France did a *volte face* from its 1982 Nationalization Act and moved after 1986 in the opposite direction by privatizing its major banks, insurance companies and large industrial groups. Similarly, Germany continued to privatize companies in the late 1980s, including the Vereinigte Electrizitaets-Und Bergwerks AG (Veba), Volkswagen, VIAG (an energy chemicals and aluminium state holding company) and Lufthansa. Italy has traditionally possessed a larger state sector with holding companies; for example, the Instituto per la Ricostruzione Industriale and the Ente Nazionale Indrocarburi, but it has started to privatize sectors such as banking, telecommunications, cars and its state airline. Spain similarly has a large state holding company, the Instituto Nacional de Industria (INI), but has encouraged some privatization, exemplified by the sale of SEAT to Volkswagen.

Privatization is beneficial mainly at a microeconomic level, with competition lowering costs and prices. Its main drawback is simply turning monopolies from public to private ownership. At a macroeconomic level privatization provides some governmental gain in reducing its expenditure and generating income from the sale of assets. However, a major consequence of privatization is shedding jobs on a large scale to make companies profitable to sell and further pruning by private management later. It may be argued that in state hands there was overmanning, disguised unemployment and low productivity. Nevertheless, the problem created is one of mass redundancies with the failure of many of the unemployed with specific skills to find new employment.

An example of the ultimate privatization in the UK has been seen in the coal industry following the privatization of power generators which sought the lowest cost source of supply, with a 'dash to gas'. The coal industry in the UK has had to shed labour and raise productivity to compete with low cost coal imports. Further new redundancies may be necessary to secure new contracts from the electricity generators in 1998. Certainly employment can never be maintained permanently since pits have resources which will inevitably become exhausted. But privatization has decimated employment, more so in the peripheral coalfields. The mainstay of the British coal industry is likely to remain in the Yorkshire and Nottinghamshire coalfields, now in the hands of R.J. Budge.

Privatization destroys the economic planning associated with nationalization. Jobs are lost on a large scale. Privatization of rail services reduces the scope for cross-subsidization in more remote regions. Similarly, in western Scotland it is recognized that ferries to the islands have a public service function. Proposed privatization of rail services in the UK has created additional uncertainty in the railway engineering industry supplying rolling stock. If new coaches last 30–35 years and franchises are only up to seven years, this discourages the placing of new orders. The Single Market has opened up national public procurement which has already led to restructuring in the supply industry into larger cross-national company groupings. British Rail has decided to defer new orders until the late 1990s, despite the recognition that new coaches are needed for commuters such as those in the south-east of England. The consequence is plant closures, with political uncertainty over the future of a privatized or nationalized railway network in the UK being likely to plague investment plans for the late 1990s.

LONG WAVES

The depth of the recession in the EU in recent years has led some economists away from short-term analysis to re-examine a long-run explanation for its continued severity. This has manifested itself in a return to the analysis of long waves, which consist of approximately 50 year business cycles: these were first proposed most forcibly by N. Kondratieff in 1926. He analysed data from the UK, France and the USA which related to prices, wages, interest rates, bank deposits, foreign trade, coal, iron and steel production (in England), and coal consumption. At the time he was writing there had been three long waves. The first of these was from the 1780s to the early 1840s; the second from the early 1840s to the late 1890s; and the third from the late 1890s to the late 1930s. A fourth cycle ran from the late 1930s up to the present time. We are now (mid 1990s) at the beginning of a fifth Kondratieff cycle.

There can be no doubt that business cycles exist and one can interpret the data empirically, if one is so minded, to yield Kondratieff cycles. However, the evidence for them is not overwhelming and in the 19th century there was far more of a boom and upswing than a down-swing (Harris, 1985). Also, the focus mainly on price movements has been distorted by inflation post-1945, with no price falls accompanying periods of stagnant output and high unemployment.

What was missing from Kondratieff's work was a coherent theoretical explanation of why such cycles occurred. This was provided subsequently by Schumpeter in terms of risk-taking entrepreneurs (Schumpeter, 1939). During recessions there is a cluster of new inventions, but according to Schumpeter what is important is their application through innovation. Once a few entrepreneurs have done this successfully in the same industry they are followed by others. Entrepreneurs innovate each time to overcome a falling rate of profit, continuing the cyclical nature of capitalism: despite some gloomy predictions the investment in innovation is sufficient to prevent the collapse of the capitalist system.

In the mid 1970s Mensch provided a fuller explanation along similar lines to Schumpeter (Mensch, 1979). He identified the peaks of innovation in particular years such as 1764, 1820, 1886 and 1935, forecasting 1989 as another radical year for innovation. Innovations are inversely related to profits and bunched during depression. However, it is still difficult to accept completely Mensch's distinction between the important basic innovations and those which improve existing products and processes. Whereas Schumpeter saw innovations bunching in particular industries, Mensch saw them taking place across industries, since in a depression firms have had to overcome their aversion to risk in order to survive. Firms also apply existing inventions more readily to try to promote recovery in profitability. However, there is still room for scepticism on dating inventions/innovations so precisely and why they should result in an upturn lasting two or more decades (Harris, 1985, p. 21).

The renewed interest in Kondratieff cycles has arisen because the early years of post-war boom (and in which the original six EC members were able to share) has given way to a more depressed performance since the early 1970s with higher unemployment. Whilst the latter fortunately has not been on the scale of the 1930s, it has jolted people's expectations. It has led to more focus on the issue of innovation *per se* and EU finance for this, plus recognition of the location of the major R&D centres. This has led some writers to be particularly gloomy about older industrial areas being capable of regenerating themselves where they lack a proper R&D base and good university facilities (Hall, 1981). Nevertheless, this may be too pessimistic a view. Whilst the growth of the microelectronic industry in California has rested on R&D, it has led to the decentralization of actual production to older industrial areas both in the USA and overseas (Marshall, 1987, p. 234).

A key feature of specialization these days is that it concerns not so much *inter*-industry specialization, but favours *intra*-industry specialization. Control, R&D and higher management is in central metropoles. The microelectronics industry in the M4 corridor in southern England is based mainly on R&D in indigenous companies, whereas in Scotland it is based more on branch plant assembly of foreign multinationals.

The upturn into the fifth Kondratieff cycle may begin in the mid to late 1990s or at the latest at the start of the new millennium (Dawson, 1993, pp. 77–8). The new bunch of innovations which have been taking place since the early 1970s will then shift the economy into sustained long-term growth. It will also have the benefit of a larger and more integrated Single European Market, with 15 EU countries, plus the re-opening of freer trade links with eastern Europe.

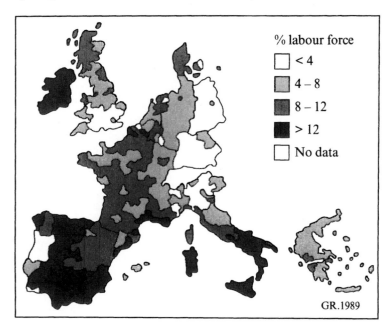

Source: *Eurostat*, Luxembourg: *OOPEC*, 1991.

Figure 2.5   EU regional unemployment rates, 1990

CHARACTERISTICS OF UNEMPLOYMENT IN THE EU

Propensity to unemployment varies according to features such as industry, employer (private or public), age, gender, ethnicity and region. The main focus, however, of the ESF and, more particularly, of the European Regional Development Fund (ERDF), is on regional unemployment.

EU regional unemployment for 1990 is shown in Figure 2.5. By the end of 1990, after the economic recovery of the late 1980s, unemployment had fallen back to just over 8 per cent. This was spread very unevenly between member states, with a marked concentration in Ireland (both north and south), large parts of Spain, the Mezzogiorno and the extreme south of France. Unemployment in these areas was over 12 per cent. By comparison, unemployment in southern Germany, northern Italy and the south of England was less than 4 per cent. Also, much of the unemployment in the EU was long term, particularly in the more depressed areas, but as a whole over half the unemployed had been out of work for one year or more. During the 1990s, unemployment has

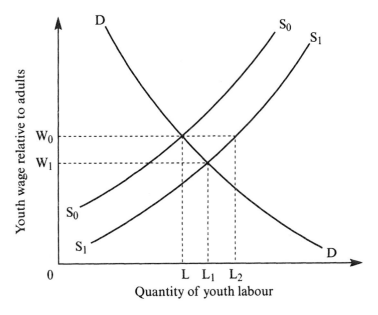

Figure 2.6   Disequilibrium in the youth labour market

risen again in the EU to 8.8 per cent in 1991, 9.5 per cent in 1992 and 11.5 per cent in 1993.

Unemployment amongst young people is excessive and very sensitive to cyclical factors, and though it tends to fall rapidly during economic recovery it rises disproportionately during recession. Youth unemployment arises since demographic factors lead to an increase in the number of young people available for work. These shift the supply of labour to the right, as shown in Figure 2.6. As with other types of unemployment, unless the market clears due to lower wages, then the result is unemployment. For example, wages may remain stuck at their original level, W_0, and demand only allows employment, 0L. There is an excess supply of young people, shown by the distance L to L_2. If only wages were more flexible and fell to $0W_1$, then demand for young people's labour would rise, with a lowering of youth unemployment. Employers have often claimed that they are unable to afford wages and the costs of training labour as well, particularly when marginal product is low during training.

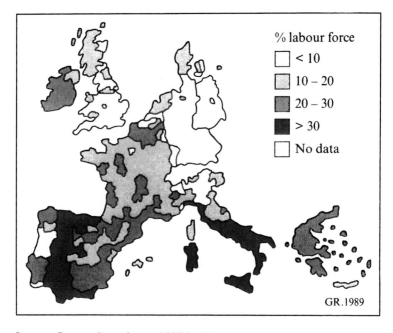

Source: *Eurostat*, Luxembourg: OOPEC, 1991.

Figure 2.7   EU regional youth unemployment rates, 1990

Table 2.1   Unemployment rates in Spain, April 1993

Level 1 Level 11	Territorial units (NUTS)	Total	Men	Women	Age <25	Age >25
SPAIN		**21.3**	**17.7**	**28.0**	**37.1**	**17.3**
Noroeste		**17.8**	**14.9**	**22.7**	**35.8**	**14.6**
Galicia		17.0	14.6	20.6	31.5	14.5
Asturias		19.6	15.4	27.0	45.5	14.7
Cantabria		19.2	15.1	26.9	38.1	15.4
Noreste		**18.6**	**13.8**	**27.6**	**36.9**	**14.9**
Pais Vasco		22.3	17.2	31.8	45.8	17.6
Navarra		12.5	8.8	19.6	20.5	10.9
La Rioja		13.6	9.4	23.0	26.8	10.9
Aragon		15.3	10.8	23.9	29.6	12.4
Madrid		**16.5**	**13.8**	**21.3**	**29.7**	**13.5**
Centro		**21.0**	**15.8**	**32.0**	**37.0**	**17.0**
Castilla y Leon		19.2	13.5	30.6	39.9	14.9
Castilla-La Mancha		18.6	14.5	28.0	29.6	15.3
Extremadura		28.9	23.2	41.0	43.3	24.9
Este		**19.6**	**15.8**	**26.0**	**34.0**	**15.7**
Cataluña		18.0	14.4	24.1	32.5	14.1
Comunidad Valenciana		22.8	18.5	30.5	37.0	18.8
Baleares		15.7	13.8	18.7	28.7	12.7
Sur		**29.7**	**26.6**	**35.8**	**44.8**	**24.8**
Andalucia		30.8	27.9	36.7	45.8	26.1
Murcia		23.4	19.5	30.6	39.1	18.2
Ceuta y Melilla		21.9	14.3	37.0	45.7	16.5
Canarias		**26.7**	**22.6**	**34.2**	**40.7**	**22.6**

Source: *Eurostat*, Luxembourg: OOPEC, 1994.

Youth unemployment, though falling rapidly in the late 1980s, was still very high in 1990. For example, youth unemployment in Spain fell from 48 per cent in 1985 to 32 per cent in 1990. Youth unemployment is shown in Figure 2.7. Apart from Spain it is high in the Mezzogiorno and the Republic of Ireland. Against a background of rising unemployment generally in the 1990s, youth unemployment in the EU rose from 14.5 per cent in 1990 to 19 per cent by May 1993. In Spain, unemployment for those under 25 years of age had risen to 37.1 per cent and in the worst hit regions reached 45 per cent. This is shown in Table 2.1.

It will be shown, for example, in Chapters 3 and 5, that whilst unemployment is an important indicator of regional problems, the EU also uses additional dimensions, especially low GDP per capita. Whilst the regions affected are largely similar on both indicators; for example, very heavy unemployment in Spain and southern Italy and low GDP per capita, there are also some differences. The two poorest countries, Portugal and Greece, with the lowest GDP per capita in the EU, have not suffered the same degree of heavy unemployment. Meanwhile, some of the declining industrial regions have been afflicted by heavy unemployment, but because they have already reached, and passed, a sufficient threshold of development, they are not characterized by such low GDP per capita. Chapter 3 moves on to a fuller coverage of these different categories of regions.

3. Regional categories and spatial inequalities

TYPES OF REGION

Regions can be classified in many ways, but to simplify here are divided into four broad categories (compare with Vickerman, 1992 and Williams, 1994). The four categories selected are: underdeveloped peripheral regions; declining and old industrial regions; core regions; and finally the newly emergent model regions of rapid technological growth (the new technopoles). Since agriculture occurs in rich and poor areas, but is more significant in poor areas, it is subsumed in this chapter in the section on underdeveloped peripheral regions, where it is a major feature. Agriculture *per se* is given greater coverage separately in the next chapter.

The main emphasis is on the problem regions, and it can be argued that these might be aggravated by the dynamic growth in core regions and in technopoles. Whilst it is true that expanding regions will tend to buy from other regions, those who adhere to a zero sum approach tend to see expansion in some regions taking place at the expense of others; for example, this may be the case where regions are competing for inward investment, and if this locates in core areas, then their gain is largely the loss experienced by the periphery.

Underdeveloped Peripheral Regions

In the original EC of six member states, underdeveloped peripheral regions were exemplified partly by the existing border regions of most countries, but after integration many such regions became central. One exception was the eastern border of western Germany which only became more central in the 1990s after the re-unification of the two Germanys. The other main exception was the south of Italy because of the very marked regional dualism between north and south. This continues to exist, with the main change being faster developments in central Italy (for example, through successful SMEs), giving rise to the wish by some writers to re-divide into three Italys.

It was the first and second enlargements of the EC which added greatly to the number and scale of underdeveloped peripheral regions, which now include whole countries: Ireland, Portugal, Spain and Greece. These countries have higher dependence on agricultural employment than elsewhere in the EU. They have been supportive of the EU because of Common Agricultural Policy (CAP) expenditure, plus the growth in their structural funding. Their growth performance in the EU has varied, with Greece doing worst, its economic growth rate since accession being significantly poorer than previously. Greece has benefited less from foreign investment than others and is relatively uncompetitive, apart from its traditional sectors such as footwear, clothing and textiles. Greece also suffers from having no common border with other EU states and therefore is vulnerable to transport difficulties caused by outside disorder, for example, in the former Yugoslavia. Despite plans for better road transport, more secure transport developments could be achieved through consolidating its strong shipping sector and upgrading its aviation links.

Ireland had a promising start and grew well in the late 1970s. It has a stronger educational system and a more skilled labour force than the southern European countries. It also differs from them in having a much stronger performance in technological sectors, mainly because of its success in attracting foreign investment. It shows vulnerable overdependence on this score and the SEM is likely to increase further foreign inward investment. However, many of its indigenous industries and firms have gone through restructuring and downsizing, and more recently the gap between Ireland and the EU has widened. Ireland's problems are exacerbated by its isolation from the EU, with transport difficulties adding to delivery costs. The main EU transport developments are passing it by; therefore, to provide closer links with the EU, attention needs to be given to developments in telecommunications.

Spain, which was doing less well before accession to the EC in 1986, has done much better post-1986 and its industrial base has widened. Portugal, which was doing well before and is stronger in more traditional industrial sectors, has had an even better performance. Foreign investment flows into Spain and Portugal increased, for example, during 1984–88 from less than 0.5 per cent of GDP in both Spain and Portugal to 1.5 per cent in Spain and nearly 2.5 per cent in Portugal. Nevertheless, there remains a marked regional disparity between the poor interior of Portugal and the more developed coastal regions, which account for more than four-fifths of the total population, with heavy concentration in the industrial areas such as Lisbon and Oporto.

The gap between the core regions and the underdeveloped peripheral regions remains wide. The latter are still highly dependent on the former for inward investment by multinational companies. Also, they have low service employment, apart from sectors such as tourism. Continued emigration of labour has helped to alleviate problems of unemployment and to supply remittances home. Nevertheless, rates of unemployment have remained persistently high, especially in Ireland and Spain.

Declining and Old Industrial Regions

These exist in the traditional regions which were the first to industrialize. They are exemplified by parts of northern Britain, Wallonia in Belgium and the German Ruhr. With the re-unification of Germany, areas such as Saxony can be included, since a lack of competitiveness in heavy and often polluting industries has resulted in their contraction under the new market system.

The traditional staple industries such as coal, iron and steel, and textiles have contracted. They have faced intense competition from new products and from new sources of supply, such as the NICs. Those regions which have adapted best, such as the Ruhr, have been in countries with a strong industrial performance and where location has been fairly central. In contrast, in the Wallonian area of Belgium, restructuring was less effective since, for cultural and linguistic reasons trying to maintain more balanced treatment, Wallonia did not receive the full regional aid which was merited on regional economic grounds. Instead, Flanders with its advantages of deep water harbours and a less unionized workforce proved far more attractive to new industrial development. It was partly to tackle the disadvantaged south that NATO was persuaded to move its strategic military headquarters (SHAPE) to Mons (whilst the political organization is in Brussels).

The process of de-industrialization has wrought havoc in many old industrial areas, displacing workers in the same way that agricultural change had done earlier. The UK, the first to industrialize and the first to de-industrialize, has suffered far more heavily than others, such as Germany or France, from the decline in industrial employment. Countries which have suffered least from this process are those such as Italy which have been more successful in maintaining their share of world exports of manufactured goods. Italy has also proved itself very flexible in coping with changes in sectors such as textiles with its versatile SMEs, often on the fringe of the 'black' economy. The key issue is the extent to which de-industrialization causes economic problems. Clearly, industries in a mature phase have to restructure, and provided productivity rises sufficiently to maintain competitiveness and raise overall output, this could be regarded as successful readaptation. Labour is shaken out and is available for re-employment in other more dynamic sectors.

The problem is that regions suffering from a high degree of industrial localization and failing to attract new dynamic industries are left with a pool of unemployed labour, often elderly and lacking new skills. Furthermore, they are often immobile not just occupationally and industrially within the region, but also geographically relatively immobile. In relation to the latter much hinges on the housing tenure composition with the privately rented sector being most conducive to labour mobility. In the UK, for example, this has fallen from around 90 per cent of housing in 1900 down to around 10 per cent today.

Whilst the debate has generally been conducted at national level about de-industrialization and key sectors, there is no doubt that the regional impact has been devastating. For example, a comparative study between machine tool companies in West Yorkshire and other continental countries showed that the least successful companies were the ones which failed to innovate; for example, those slow to add computer numerical control to their machines were the ones to fare worst. British firms were often in more down-market products, such as basic lathes, where the competition from NICs was at its fiercest. Other countries were often better able to adapt because of a superior multi-skilled workforce, as in Germany.

Certainly the sectors regarded historically as key sectors: agriculture (by the Physiocrals) and industry (by Kaldor, amongst others, because of its fast productivity rise) now employ a much diminished workforce compared with the growth of the service sector (Kaldor, 1966). Whilst the latter offers greater stability, it also tends to employ more women (especially on a part-time basis), whilst the former industrial employees (mainly men) often remain unemployed for long periods. Some writers have bemoaned the growth of the non-market sector (Bacon and Eltis, 1976), and this may have been an additional catalyst for privatization. Nevertheless, the fact remains that the pattern of employment has changed enormously towards the service sector, though not in the sense of personal servants, whose numbers have declined during this century as egalitarianism has progressed. Income and price elasticities of demand are higher for services, which is where comparative advantage now lies for some regions. Unfortunately for the older industrial regions, it is other regions which tend to have comparative advantage in supplying services. Furthermore, to the extent that the SEM focuses on opening up the sale of services even more, it is probably the existing core areas which may benefit most.

Core Regions

Core regions are generally based on major capital cities where there has been a rapid accumulation of capital. In addition, the rapid growth has provided a magnetic attraction to labour to move into core areas to find work. For example, Paris is a major European and world city, with about 20 per cent of the French population living in this region. It was assumed by J.F. Gravier (1947) in his book, *Paris et le Désert Français*, that Paris would continue to grow and create an economic desert elsewhere. This has not materialized, though Paris has grown through suburban poles of new town development. Capital cities have not been immune to the problems of declining employment in manufacturing industry and attempts to decentralize activity.

Urban problems have arisen, particularly in the inner city. In London, for example, the Docklands Development Corporation has tried to revive the East End with office buildings and financial services. Local people claim that the main beneficiaries have been the new institutions which have moved in, often displacing the local residents who found it more and more costly to live there.

Europe's capital cities are increasingly in competition with one another for the location of new institutional headquarters. London, for example, was successful in strengthening its claim to be Europe's premier financial centre with the setting up there of the European Bank for Reconstruction and Development. This confirms the city's continued role as an exporter of capital, in this case to eastern Europe. Other continental cities have major aspirations to consolidate their own role as more significant financial centres, such as Frankfurt, which has been chosen as the base for the EU's new Central Bank.

Capital cities in core regions have enormous advantages from agglomeration, skilled labour and the convergence of transport networks.

In addition, they have the stability provided by the growth of a large service sector, particularly in governmental employment. Perhaps their main difficulty lies in congestion and in trying to devise an appropriate mix of public/private transport to alleviate this problem. Certainly those cities which are best able to invest in new and superior infrastructure will possess an added advantage in the future. Brussels is now clearly recognized as the capital of the EU. Meanwhile, the redesignation of Berlin as the capital of a united Germany is refocusing location activities eastwards.

Rapidly Developing Technopole Regions

These may be located close to a core region or some distance from it. They are new industrial areas based on modern technologies which have benefited from a pleasant environment, modern transport facilities and new purpose-built premises. They are often characterized by close links with a prestigious university and the creation of science parks which have led to the commercial application of new inventions. This has led to the nurturing of new SMEs.

France provides good examples of such developments since it was a pioneer in the creation of growth poles in completely new sectors based on the achievement of a critical R&D mass. Apart from Nice and Montpellier, Grenoble occupies a special successful position in the Rhône-Alpes region: some of Europe's most advanced industries and scientific research centres are based there. Its rapid expansion has been stimulated by effective links between its universities and local industries. It has also been underpinned by the mountainous terrain providing not only attractive scenery, but also a source of hydroelectric power. This has attracted new people who have poured in, as in California, providing dynamic new developments (Ardagh, 1982, pp. 153–61). Grenoble has grown to some 1 per cent of the French population but provides about 10 per cent of French R&D employment (Vickerman, 1992, p. 174). The Rhône-Alpes region has benefited greatly from the willingness of the French to invest in new transport infrastructure on a far more ambitious scale than their counterparts in the UK. In particular, France has been more supportive of rail transport, with its high speed trains (TGVs) making great inroads into travelling times to major cities, such as Lyons.

In south-east England, areas close to the universities of Oxford and Cambridge, and along new motorway links from London, have become attractive fresh poles of development. The M40 to Oxford and the M4 running west from London past Swindon have encouraged high-tech firms to locate there.

On the continent, technopole developments may lead to a new core of successful development from southern Germany, south-east France, north-west Italy and north-east Spain. If regional inequalities in other problem regions are to be tackled effectively, a similar policy will need to be pursued by the EU to create and foster technopoles. Since the likelihood of these arising spontaneously in the problem regions is very remote, the EU needs to finance the establishment of new R&D centres in less developed regions (Holland, 1993, p. 222).

RATIONALE FOR NATIONAL AND COMMUNITY REGIONAL POLICY

National Regional Policies

A combination of geographical, economic, social and political factors all underpin national regional policies. Geographically there are vast differences in population density, with benefits to be gained from a less skewed distribution of population and land use. However, to the extent that governmental intervention is feasible to modify the existing pattern in the location of economic activities, much rests on the degree to which these are now footloose. Certainly industries are no longer tied as in the past to local sources of power, and transport these days is far superior. Although it might be argued by critics that some examples of government intervention to relocate industries have been unsuccessful, such as the motor industry in Scotland, the general case of the European motor industry shows that production facilities can be widely dispersed.

National economic management is concerned to promote a better rate of economic growth which in turn will reduce the level of unemployment. There is a marked under-utilization of resources, reflected in higher regional levels of unemployment and low activity rates in weaker regions. Regional policy provides a tool to improve not just regional economic performance but in so doing enhances national economic performance. However, these advantages were most apparent during the 1960s when national economies were short of labour and very active regional policies were pursued. Since the 1970s depressed economic performance has led not only to high rates of regional unemployment but a major problem nationally of unemployment. The magnitude of national unemployment has tended to overwhelm governments, leading them in turn to lose sight of some individual regional difficulties. It has been recognized that not only has unemployment spread more widely, but in absolute terms there are far more people unemployed in some of the large cities in the core regions. Also, many of the unemployed there possess a better range of skills than are found in the older industrial regions. Nevertheless, the facts are that activity rates are lower and structural long-term unemployment remains heavier in the weaker regions.

Governmental economic policy has become one of trying to root out unacceptably high levels of inflation. With a worse trade-off between unemployment and inflation, inflation begins to pick up rapidly, for example, in the UK once unemployment drops below about two and a quarter million. However, in confronting inflation, regional policy provides an additional policy instrument, albeit a relatively minor one. When expansionist economic policy is concentrated in areas which are already congested, such as the core regions, then wages, rents and prices all rise rapidly. If a similar expansion were redirected to the weaker and less prosperous regions, where supply is more elastic, then output would increase with a minimal inflationary consequence.

On social grounds there is a strong case that in equity all regions should participate and benefit from economic development and progress. The degree to which central government accepts this argument will depend partly on whether it is dependent on electoral support in the area and also the degree to which it enables central government to alleviate its political overload (Keating and Jones, 1985).

Politically, in Germany and Italy a deliberate regional policy was pursued post-1945 to prevent any re-emergence of totalitarian power. Central governments have been prepared to cede some power to their regions because of distinctive differences, such as language or culture. They have feared the alternative scenario which might consist of even greater pressure for regional secession and ultimately a complete split, with separate autonomy.

The case for national regional policies is straightforward, and more significant is the vigour with which these have been pursued and the different types of policy which have been favoured. National regional policies were at their most active from the late 1950s up to the early 1970s. Before that time the main concern was with national economic recovery and growth, to which regional policy was subservient. After the early 1970s regional problems were overtaken by national economic problems as recession affected all regions. Hence the vogue for controls in congested areas diminished, whereas this had been favoured by the UK for London, by France for Paris, and also in the Netherlands and in Italy. It was the latter which experienced the most severe regional dualism and was the only country which operated a labour subsidy, through the social security system, once the UK abandoned its regional employment premium. Now there are more labour-related schemes to tackle higher unemployment, with the UK having a useful system with its Regional Development grant being either a grant per job or a capital grant depending on which is most favourable for the applicant. Apart from Italy, Ireland also enjoyed a very extensive range of national measures. Yuill, Allen and Hull (eds) (1980) identified 25 major regional incentives used by member states, with the five main types being interest-related subsidies (the principal element of Belgian and Danish policies), tax concessions, depreciation allowances, labour subsidies and, most importantly, capital grants. The trend more recently has been towards grants and away from soft loans. In the smaller countries such as Belgium, Denmark and Luxembourg, policy was highly discretionary. Discretionary aid has become more fashionable since it has the advantage of cutting costs, but has the disadvantage of being unpredictable. In the Netherlands a sensible approach combines automatic aid up to a fixed amount beyond which it becomes discretionary. It has also been suggested that another improvement would be to provide automatic assistance for smaller firms and discretionary help for larger ones (Yuill and Allen in Albrechts *et al.*, 1989).

The most sophisticated planning system was built up in France which tried to develop *metropole d'équilibre* to counter the magnetic over-attraction of the Paris region. Except for the UK, other countries such as Italy, the Netherlands, Germany and Spain have also pursued policies to develop growth points, but eventually have been forced by political opposition towards more diffused coverage. In the Netherlands the over-concentration in the Randstadt has been even more pronounced than in south-east England or in Paris. Consequently the Dutch in the early post-war years switched from a labour mobility policy towards a positive regional policy, tied closely to a concept of physical planning.

In the UK separate regional development agencies have been a big help in improving the relative position of Scotland and Wales compared with English regions. The agencies have had an integrated approach and been pro-active, especially in attracting inward investment. They have had high visibility to attract new firms and to provide continued financial support, even running counter to the Conservative government's philosophy of cutting public funding for industry in general. The Welsh Development Agency in its three year plan in 1995 proposed an annual budget of £153 million, targeting £1.6 billion of new inward investment over the three years 1995–97. Certainly Wales and Scotland have become more successful than northern England, though success is relative, more so in the eastern part of Wales, for example, and also in eastern Scotland based upon the oil industry. A strategy followed particularly successfully by UK regions has been to attract inward investment. For example, Wales has attracted some 20 per cent of all inward investment into the UK; also, since 1986 some 370 foreign companies have established themselves in north-east England, creating more than 34,000 jobs. There are advantages and disadvantages. It brings in large capital investment, often with one firm following another. The wave of American and Japanese investment from outside is likely to be followed in the future from other sources such as Korea. Korean companies have set up recently in Belgium and now Samsung have chosen to produce excavating equipment in the UK. This follows swiftly from an anti-dumping complaint lodged against it by European manufacturers. It has chosen to locate in a part of North Yorkshire which does not qualify it for regional selective assistance, but has good infrastructure and is close to the A1 road network. However, a downside of inward investment is that often the jobs created are not numerous, are unstable (with the uncertain branch plant syndrome) and are often low paid and relatively unskilled jobs; the main R&D activity tending to be retained elsewhere and outside peripheral regions.

As the competition for inward investment hots up between regions inside and outside Europe, then a question mark has to be placed over regional policies which rely too much upon inward investment. The case of Wales has been compared unfavourably in some respects with development in regions elsewhere in the EU, such as the Basque country where development has been based more on indigenous support for SMEs and help with new technology (Rees and Morgan in Day and Rees (eds), 1994). In the Basque region the machine tool industry has been nurtured more successfully than in the UK, with a successful cooperative system, incorporation of the latest computer numerically controlled technology and successful exports to major markets such as Germany and the USA. However, having said all that, Welsh strategy has been much more effective in bringing down unemployment compared with the very high levels which exist in Spain.

Marked regional disparities exist, with north–south problems in Italy, Belgium and the UK, though in the latter it is the north which is most depressed. In other countries the problems are more east–west, as in the Netherlands and Ireland, with western Ireland being depressed compared with eastern parts. However, there is a danger of over-generalization since there are areas of prosperity even in depressed regions. For example, in southern Italy there is some congestion in particular cities, whilst in the depressed Walloon area of Belgium pockets of relative prosperity exist. Overall, prior to re-unification the least problems regionally were in west Germany, which achieved strong economic growth at a national level and regional balance through the *Länder*. It had no need to control a major capital city and its problems were mainly at a sub-regional level. This has now changed, with re-unification absorbing the eastern *Länder* whose former low unemployment has given way to massive unemployment. Luxembourg remains the main beacon of prosperity, being too small to have major regional divisions. However, when some countries offered strong regional policy incentives, others were forced to follow suit until the EC introduced its own policy.

Enlargement of the EU has increased the focus on southern Europe, with Spain, for example, in the early post-war period facing similar problems to southern Italy. Whereas the latter made full use of its large state holding companies, forcing them to locate at least 60 per cent of all their new investments in the Mezzogiorno, Spain did not use the INI in the same way. Spain has experienced marked over-concentration on the Madrid–Basque country and Catalan triangle. Under the Franco dictatorship emphasis was on highly centralized national policy, but the political transition to democracy in Spain has now had to meet the historic claims for autonomy by the Basques and the Catalans. These claims were recognized in the Spanish constitution in 1978, with the extension of regional government to Spanish regions (F. Morata in Leonardi (ed.), 1993, p. 187). Similarly, in Portugal the change from dictatorship has reduced the amount of central control seen to be necessary over actual and potential local opposition. Enhanced regional power has been encouraged further by the EU through input into the Community Support Framework (CSF). The latter leads on to the next section, looking more fully at the case for EU regional policy.

EU Regional Policy

Clearly the rationale of a regional policy at a national level is intertwined and overlaps with that of an EU regional policy. In addition to the basic elements underlying regional policy, the argument for the EU's role is based on specific features. The Thomson Report talked about a moral case for EC regional policy since, 'no community could maintain itself nor have a meaning for the peoples which belong to it as long as some have very different standards of living and have cause to doubt the common will of all to help each Member to better the conditions of its people' (CEC, 1973, p. 4).

Whilst a market promotes increased efficiency which is potentially beneficial to all, in the short run there are losers who need to be given compensation. A Pareto improvement would consist of a lump sum transfer on a once-and-for-all basis to those who were losers, and behaviourally it would be non-distorting. The EU philosophy is simpler than the Pareto approach since it helps those relatively poorly off to adjust (Bliss (ed.), 1990, p. 371). The aim is to assist the weaker regions to catch up by equalizing their resource endowment. Hence the purpose is not to eliminate all inequalities, but to offer the opportunities to do so.

From the viewpoint of an effective deployment of resources, these should be concentrated on the areas with the most severe regional problems in the EU. Without EU intervention national governments will aid their own weaker regions, and yet the poorest regions of a rich member state are often richer than the richest regions of a poor EU member state. Therefore it is equitable, given that we are all European citizens, to concentrate assistance on the poorest EU regions. Since the poorest regions tend to lie in the poorest member states, a greater level of expenditure can only be concentrated there by redistribution from the financial resources of the richer member states. Although the feeling of citizenship is still likely to be less at the EU level than at the national level, the EU can mobilize increased resources to tackle regional problems. The EU can oversee a bigger level of regional expenditure and give a sharper focus to it.

The EU may in some respects be adding to regional disparities; for example, its largest and most important source of expenditure is on agriculture. Yet the non-Objective 1 regions have obtained up to 24 times as much per worker from the European Agricultural Guidance and Guarantee Fund (EAGGF) expenditure than all of Greece, most of

Spain and Portugal, the Mezzogiorno and parts of southern France (Holland, 1993, p. 186). The more open trading policy is also putting pressure on less competitive firms and industries, particularly in weaker regions, not only in competition from other member states, but also from third countries. Although the EU's common industrial policy deals with both sunset and sunrise industries, its finance for new high-tech industries further reinforces regional imbalance. This is because most R&D work is concentrated in the most prosperous and developed areas by a few major successful firms. Twelve major firms in central urban areas have accounted for up to 70 per cent of Community research budgets. For example, in the European Strategic Programme for Research and Development in Information Technology (ESPRIT) expenditure in 1987, from 200 programmes of co-operation only one firm from Spain's Objective 1 regions participated, along with 13 firms from Portugal, 20 firms from Greece and only seven firms from Italy's Objective 1 regions. A similar regional maldistribution has been found to exist in other EU industrial programmes, such as BRITE (Holland, 1993, p. 190).

The process of integration is removing many national policies, such as state support to particular sectors which infringe EU competition policy within the SEM. Furthermore, not only are microeconomic policies in many sectors being shifted upwards to EU competency, but also macroeconomic policies. EMU further constrains the ability to depreciate exchange rates to enable less competitive firms, industries and regions within weaker economies to compete effectively.

CONVERGENT AND DIVERGENT REGIONAL TRENDS IN THE EU

The growth of free trade enables areas to specialize in those products in which they have a comparative advantage. They concentrate on producing and exporting products in which they have an abundant factor endowment. Those well endowed with labour, for example, will export labour-intensive products, thereby raising wage rates. Furthermore, the EU is characterized not only by free trade but also by free factor mobility. Where wage differences still exist on any significant level, labour will have the incentive and opportunity to emigrate. Likewise capital will flow into areas where it can take advantage of low costs of labour and land. Multinational companies in particular may be considered as a new and potent influence on the pattern of regional development since many of them practise a spatial international division of labour in their operations; for example, by establishing labour-intensive production in poor regions.

Empirically one can find some limited evidence to support convergence both between weaker and richer member states of the EU and between their weaker regions. In examining convergence/divergence there are three particular issues of concern. The first relates to the indicators to be used in measurement; for example, GDP per capita and unemployment. The second issue is the level to which these are to be applied: between countries, between regions within each member state, or between regions across the EU. The third issue concerns the time period which is covered. Essentially the key issue is the extent to which a balance can be achieved between the core regions in the EU and others, especially the more peripheral ones. Core regions of prosperity are located down from southern England through Flanders and Randstadt-Holland/Limburg; western Germany, south-eastern France and on into northern Italy.

It should also be emphasized that the focus here is on real convergence. It therefore departs from the conventional wisdom embodied in the Maastricht Treaty, which emphasizes nominal macroeconomic convergence. Whilst this convergence in elements such as inflation is crucial in sustaining a durable EMU, it does not automatically guarantee real convergence. There is a painful short-run shock adjustment to reduce inflationary pressures, reflected in high unemployment. This was as true in the 1930s as today, with low inflation *per se* being no guarantee of economic recovery; it simply provides a platform from which this can be undertaken subsequently.

The main indicator usually used is that of GDP per capita, generally expressed as purchasing power parity to cover an identical volume of goods and services, taking into account differences in price levels. In addition, one can also compare unemployment percentages. If these indicators are applied firstly to disparities between countries, one can begin on a fairly optimistic note. During the golden period of rapid economic growth in the post-war period there were converging trends. The countries at a lower level of economic development, such as Italy, began to catch up and were able to use not just new technology but the backlog of technological innovations. Countries such as Germany recovered and reconstructed, growing more rapidly economically than the highly developed United Kingdom which grew relatively slowly.

Table 3.1 *A comparison of national GDP per capita, 1980–90*

Country	GDP per capita (purchasing power parity) Eur = 100	
	1980	1990
Greece	52	47
Spain	72	75
France	114	112
Portugal	53	56
UK	97	101
Ireland	61	68
Italy	102	102
Luxembourg	115	124
Denmark	106	107
Germany	119	117
Belgium	106	105
Netherlands	108	101

Source: *Eurostat,* Luxembourg: *OOPEC,* 1993.

Indeed, in the case of the UK this is not just a post-1945 phenomenon but dates from the late 19th century.

EU enlargement has been a crucial turning point in enhancing regional policy and in the 1980s the national level approach reflected the marked underdevelopment and low GDP per capita of Portugal, Greece, Spain and Ireland. It can be seen in Table 3.1, which compares national GDP per capita, that there was some convergence of the countries with the lowest GDP per capita, the major exception being Greece. As a consequence the spread of GDP per capita ranged in 1990 from 47 for Greece to 124 in Luxembourg (whose GDP per capita continued to grow rapidly). Nevertheless the majority of countries converged towards the EU average of 100.

It can be argued that the member state level is a very important one since the member state in the EU is becoming increasingly analogous to a region itself and to an American state. Some comparison with the latter is considered further at the end of this section. Also, it might be argued that most people still identify mainly with the member state as citizens in terms of their expectations and rights to welfare provision.

Using a different indicator of national economic differences, that of unemployment disparities, there was a wider spread; for example, in 1993 it ranged from Luxembourg again being best placed with 2.5 per cent unemployment, to 21.5 per cent in Spain. Also, a slightly different picture emerges of national problems when unemployment is used as the main focus instead of income per head. One puzzle to be explained is how Iberian neighbours, Spain and Portugal, differ so much in unemployment, with Portugal continuing to record low unemployment – in 1993 it was 5 per cent. Greece similarly has had relatively low unemployment. Only in the case of Spain and Ireland do the unemployment statistics reinforce the relatively low GDP per capita.

If one turns next away from the national level to the more common presentation of a region's inequalities, the case of the two Italys has reflected the most distinctive example of regional dualism since the EC's inception. The foundations of this pre-date the EC and in the early 1950s GDP per capita in the Mezzogiorno was 55 per cent of that in the north-centre. Active regional policy by state spending on agriculture, infrastructure and direct investment of nationalized holding companies has prevented the regional gap from growing. However, the gap has not narrowed much, especially in the 1980s, and by 1989 the GDP per capita ratio was 56 per cent of that in the north-centre. It is worth bearing in mind, though, that the growth of GDP per capita in northern Italy has been outstanding and the Mezzogiorno is not poor, with a GDP per capita above that of Greece, Portugal and Ireland, but below that of Spain. The southern Italian model of development, though highly approved of by some economists (Holland, 1979), is now seen largely to have failed. Although it has raised per capita private consumption in the Mezzogiorno to 69 per cent of that in the north-centre, this has compounded Italy's basic problem of budgetary deficits. Southern development has been based too much on transfers, and despite high investment, particularly by state-owned industries (though never reaching the targets set for state investment in the Mezzogiorno), productivity remains low. Wages in the Mezzogiorno are too high in relation to skill levels, with income transfers increasing workers' reservation wages, below which they are not prepared to work.

The UK also has a marked north/south divide (with a depressed north) which has a much longer history than is commonly assumed (Lewis and Townsend (eds), 1989, pp. 26–8). In the years 1911–12 per capita incomes in south-east England were three times higher than those in the periphery. The UK has experienced not only slow economic growth but a highly cyclical pattern, with export-dependent regions suffering heavily from de-industrialization. The ripple from the core to periphery has been increasingly outweighed by a bigger periphery extending southwards, leaving only the south-east of England above average in EU terms on the basis of GDP per capita. Even unemployment in the south-east is high and now above that in other parts of the UK such as Scotland and Wales. For example, at 10.5 per cent in April 1993, unemployment in south-east England was above the UK average of 10.3 per cent and higher than that in Scotland (10.1 per cent) and Wales (9.7 per cent).

The broader picture of regional trends which emerges in the EC shows a tendency for these inequalities to narrow during the 1960s and up to the 1970s, since when they have tended to widen marginally. The per capita income is roughly of the order of 2:1 between the highest and lowest region within each member state. This is shown in Table 3.2, with Ireland, Luxembourg and Denmark being excluded since these are classed as single regions.

Despite the relative improvement shown in the national performance of Portugal there has also been very clear widening between the lowest

Table 3.2   Regional GDP per capita, 1980–90

Country	GDP per capita 1980		GDP per capita 1990 (Eur = 100)	
	Lowest	Highest	Lowest	Highest
Greece	35	71	34	58
Spain	45	91	49	98
France	87	182	79	166
Portugal	44	69	35	76
UK	74	114	74	154 (121)
Italy	58	135	61	135
Germany	85	187	81	183
Belgium	83	166	78	166
Netherlands	87	208	61 (82)	135

Note: The figures in brackets for the UK and the Netherlands are those most directly comparable to 1980.

Source: *Eurostat*, OOPEC, 1993, cited in Michie and Grieve Smith (eds), 1994, p. 147.

and highest Portuguese regions; this is because most new investment was concentrated in the Lisbon/Setubal region. Widening is evident between regions in other member states such as the UK, though it should be noted that the latter still has one of the narrowest differences between its regions internally and this is also much narrower than historically. It might be argued that citizens are mainly concerned with differences between regions in the member state in which they live, since they are more aware and conscious of these through the media, travel, relatives, and so on.

However, the main focus from a policy angle is to compare inter-regional differences between member states of the lowest and highest regions. One can also compare across the EU's regions; for example, by referring back to Table 3.2 showing Germany's highest GDP per capita region at over five times more than the lowest region in Greece. Whilst this may be less relevant to the average Greek citizen than the regional difference which exists with Athens, from a policy implementation angle the argument is that aid should be concentrated only on the regions falling significantly below the EU average. Hence as EU regional policy has evolved, the structural fund criteria have placed the prime focus on inter-regional differences between member states.

One can also see that unemployment rates between regions are marked. For example, in April 1993 average unemployment in Germany was 7 per cent, ranging from 3.9 per cent in Bayern to 14.1 per cent in Mecklenburg-Vorpommern. German re-unification has contributed to much wider inter-regional differences. Another country with even wider inter-regional differences is Italy, with average unemployment of 11.2 per cent in April 1993, ranging from Lombardia at 4.5 per cent to Sicilia at 23.1 per cent. Spain, which has the highest unemployment at 21.3 per cent, ranged from 16.5 per cent in Madrid to 29.7 per cent in Sur (for example, 30.8 per cent in Andalucia). Unemployment differences within other member states tended to be narrower; for example, 10.3 per cent in the UK, ranging from 8.4 per cent in East Anglia to 15 per cent in Northern Ireland.

Spatial analysis in focusing mainly on inter-regional differences has largely ignored intra-regional differences. Yet within regions there are wide differences in incomes and unemployment levels between successful towns and cities and less successful ones. In fact, such an observation is relevant in refuting a blanket geographical explanation of spatial inequalities. In the UK, for example, there are some prosperous and successful northern towns and equally some depressed towns on the south coast and depressed parts of London. It shows that indigenous enterprise is crucial and much can be learned from examining such areas (provided one excludes those which are largely residential commuter towns for large cities, since these reflect mainly a social middle-class location).

To the extent that there has been convergence this has been strengthened by governmental policies of automatic and discretionary transfers redistributing income to weaker regions. However, the degree of convergence achieved was highest in the early years of the EU when, during the 1960s, there was a high rate of economic growth, with labour shortages inducing a high degree of emigration from weaker regions. This reduced excess supply of labour in countries of origin and alleviated labour shortages in host countries. Also, countries of origin received remittances sent back by migrant workers, helping to boost investment and improve the balance-of-payments position of the home country.

Since enlargement the growth performance of Spain and Portugal has been particularly impressive, as shown in Table 3.3, though disappointing in Greece.

Table 3.3   Relative growth performance of less developed EC countries before and after accession to the EC, 1974–90

Country	Year of accession	Before*	After
Ireland	1973	–	0.2
Greece	1981	1.1	–0.7
Spain	1986	–0.2	1.4
Portugal	1986	0.3	1.4

Note: *The average of differences in GDP growth rates of the countries considered and GDP growth rates of the EC for the relevant years (1974–80 for Greece; 1974–85 for Spain and Portugal).

Source: *European Economy*, No. 5, 1993, p. 334.

One element conducive to convergence between member states and particularly favourable to southern Europe, albeit in a dependency relationship, has been the massive growth in tourism. This is the largest industry in the EU, accounting for 5–6 per cent of GDP and 7.5 million jobs. It has helped to redistribute expenditure from richer member

Table 3.4   Tourism and regional development, 1991

	GDP/capita EC(12) = 100 1991	Ratio of travel account receipts to GDP (%)	Share of travel account receipts in exports of goods and services (%)
Greece	49	3.9	17.7
Portugal	60	6.0	15.5
Ireland	72	3.4	4.4
Spain	80	3.8	22.5
Belgium	108	1.9	1.9
Luxembourg	131		
Italy	106	1.8	6.4
Netherlands	104	1.3	2.1
UK	98	1.4	3.5
France	115	1.7	5.9
Denmark	111	2.5	5.3
Germany	106	0.7	2.1
	(formerly 114 for W. Germany)		

Sources: Column 1: Regional Trends No. 29 (HMSO) July 1994. Columns 2 and 3: OECD, Tourism Policy and International Tourism, Paris, 1992.

states to poorer member states. It has stimulated economic development, particularly in the four EU countries with GDP per capita significantly below the EU average of 100. The travel account receipts as a percentage of GDP range from 3.4 per cent in Ireland to 6 per cent in Portugal. Travel account receipts as a percentage of exports of goods and services are even higher, ranging from 15.5 per cent in Portugal to 22.5 per cent in Spain (see Table 3.4).

In addition, EU countries can also be classified according to the effects of tourism in improving the balance-of-payments position. This is done in Table 3.5, showing that, with the exception of the British Isles in 1990, tourism was beneficial, either in reducing a current account deficit in the balance of payments, particularly in southern Europe, or in reducing a current account surplus for northern European countries.

It is the poorer countries which tend to be the ones with the most severe regional problems. Within countries the richer regions, though major receivers of tourism, are net generators. Italy's three major tour-

Table 3.5   The EU tourism balance effect in 1990

Reducing the current account deficit	Reducing the current account surplus	Adding to the current account imbalance
Greece	Germany	UK
Spain	Netherlands	Ireland
Portugal	Belgium/Luxembourg	
Italy	Denmark	
France		

ist generating areas: Lombardy, Piedmont and Lazio, which account for nearly 40 per cent of Italy's GDP, generated nearly half of all vacation days, whilst all other Italian regions were net receivers of tourists (Pearce, 1987). Policy-makers have recognized the beneficial effects which tourism can provide and the need to spread these away from yet further over-concentration in capital cities. Tourism is fairly labour-intensive, helping to reduce high unemployment, particularly in areas with a predominantly low skilled workforce. It also offers job opportunities, especially for women, often on a part-time basis. Although areas would prefer more highly paid jobs in high-tech sectors, offering stable employment compared with seasonal tourist employment, the latter is beneficial and in already industrialized areas is a vast improvement environmentally on the old smoke-stack industries of the past. Tourism offers scope for both industrial and agricultural areas to market their attractions, be they industrial history in the case of the former or scenic attractions in the case of agriculture. The role of tourism in facilitating structural change in the latter is touched on at the end of Chapter 4.

Despite all the elements discussed so far which have acted to constrain and narrow spatial disparities, between 1975 and 1985 these trends unfortunately stopped and were partly reversed, with divergence occurring due to depressed economic conditions. Most regions have been affected during the downturn in the business cycle with those in the least competitive position naturally tending to suffer most. Investment is deterred because of increased riskiness, with a pronounced reduction in the flow of capital into new areas of activity. Also, with less demand for labour, particularly unskilled labour which is abundant in less developed regions, scope for migration is reduced. In fact, during recession some return migration has been evident from some countries such as Germany. With tougher economic conditions, cutbacks occur both in the private sector and the public sector (if governments seek to promote budgetary balance). With a reluctance to spend, demand drops and the weakest unfortunately tend to suffer most.

Businesses prefer to concentrate their production in well-tried areas in which they can benefit from all the external economies of scale which are available; for example, in terms of proximity of suppliers, a well-trained workforce and links with educational establishments. A strong technological and innovative base is characteristic of successful companies. Their preference is to cluster in more favourable regions, choosing them to conduct their R&D and often to base their headquarters there. Despite the increased focus on inward multinational investment as a source of development in weaker regions, most of this investment still flows mainly into richer countries and richer regions. This is because increasingly investment in the EU is concerned with capital-intensive production instead of using the labour-intensive methods made possible by the low wages of less developed regions.

The consequences are that regional divergence in the EU is still very wide, as indicated in earlier Tables using GDP per capita purchasing parity (which corrects for differences in price levels). To this can be added other observations (Vickerman, 1992, p. 54) that GDP in the two richest regions of Germany was nearly five times higher than in the two poorest Italian regions. However, regions have shown that it is possible to improve their fortunes, with some Italian regions, for example, improving their relative positions (Leonardi (ed.), 1993). Nevertheless, the improvements have not been as large as those in the USA which are reflected in vast improvements in some of the southern states, such as North Carolina and Georgia.

Regional divergence in the EU is much more marked than in the USA. For example, the Gini co-efficient can be used and has a value of between zero and one, with moves towards zero indicating greater equality and vice versa. It is useful in comparing inequality over time, and though its overall value may be unambiguous where the whole Lorenz curve shifts, it is ambiguous where there are intersecting Lorenz curves. Regional income inequality for the EU at 0.131 was calculated to be nearly twice that of the USA at 0.072 (Boltho, 1989). It can be seen that these Gini co-efficients for regional income are low, and much lower than those found for general income distribution. This is because both rich and poor households are present in differing degrees in all regions.

It is clear that the EU level of integration is newer and less deep than that in the USA. Nevertheless, an interesting fact is that the narrowing of regional income differentials in the USA is relatively recent, taking place mainly since the Second World War. High demand for labour encouraged labour mobility, which is far greater in the American labour market. By contrast, in the EU (as shown in Chapter 6), gross migration has affected only 1–1.5 per cent of the EU population and net migration between member states has fallen to negligible proportions. With the fall in demand particularly for semi- and unskilled workers, the increased movement is of skilled and professional people. This has been encouraged by EU measures to standardize and accept a mutual recognition of qualifications. Whilst migration has generally been beneficial economically, there is some worry that an exodus of skilled workers might weaken the skills base in some regions.

The EU lacks the common language and the rootlessness which helped to create the American melting pot. It seems unlikely that the EU will ever reach the same level of integration seen in the US labour market. However, member states in the EU, as in the USA, have been able to provide significant budgetary transfers within each state. In the USA these have reduced per capita income differences by some 25 per cent, and even more in the case of the UK and France. Unfortunately, these transfers have not been replicated between the member states of the EU. The small federal budget of the EU constitutes a major defect compared with the federal budget in the USA. This is preventing the necessary degree of income redistribution between member states which needs to be tackled, as enlargement meant that the regional problems which were manifest between countries have now grown in importance compared to those within countries. This issue of the budget and the particular (over)emphasis on agriculture is considered in the next chapter.

4. Budget finance for agriculture and fisheries

BUDGET REVENUE AND EXPENDITURE

The Community's existence is manifested by its own budget and this determines the amount of financing available to carry out all its policies, such as the highly desirable structural fund expenditure. Before turning to examine the important elements of expenditure, particularly agriculture and other structural fund expenditure, it is worthwhile to mention initially its sources of revenue. Since 1970 the EC has been given its own resources, including customs duties and agricultural levies, but GATT tariff-cutting rounds have reduced the dynamism of these revenue sources. In relation to assigning taxes to different levels of government, customs duties are nearly always the exclusive competence of the federal level, as in the EU. In addition, the EU has received a significant proportion of VAT receipts since VAT was adopted as the main source of indirect taxation on goods and services. The EU became overdependent upon this and, in order to create greater progressiveness in revenue contributions, a Gross National Product (GNP)-based contribution was added. The latter covers the difference between EU spending and revenue raised from other sources. Both VAT and the GNP-based component may be considered really as national components which are handed over to Brussels. The composition of revenue sources for 1993 were as follows: customs' duties, 20 per cent; agricultural and sugar levies, 3.4 per cent; VAT, 54.5 per cent; and the GNP-based contribution, 21.4 per cent (plus miscellaneous 0.7 per cent).

The budget constituted 1.20 per cent of EU GNP in 1993 and the financial perspective for 1999 is for a rise of the own resources ceiling to 1.27 per cent of EU GNP. At the Edinburgh Summit in December 1992 it was decided to reduce the share of VAT in the budget to 34.38 per cent and to raise the GNP share to 47.90 per cent by the late 1990s. This will be achieved as the maximum rate on the harmonized VAT base is lowered in equal steps from 1.4 per cent down to 1 per cent by

1999. In the future, new taxes could comprise increased environmental taxes on pollution to curb the emission of carbon dioxide.

Although a stable financial framework has been agreed until the end of the century, it remains a prickly issue regarding the pattern of its expenditure and the appropriate size of the budget. The commitment appropriations, legally committed for payment up to 1999, are shown in Table 4.1.

Whilst the increase in structural operations mainly on the structural funds plus the Cohesion Fund is far in excess of proposed CAP expenditure, the latter in absolute terms will still be significantly in excess of spending on structural operations. Basically, the EU budget is relatively too small and currently amounts to 1.2 per cent of Community GDP, compared with an average of 48 per cent of GDP of national spending by member states. EU budgetary expenditure has been similar in size to that of the education budget or to German spending on the eastern *Länder*, or less than 10 per cent of US spending on defence. The budget also has to have an accounting balance, unlike functional national budgets which, post-Keynes, have tended to be unbalanced. The EU budget cannot run deficits in times of slump and therefore does not play a stabilization role; it also lacks flexibility as a result of its multi-annual programming. If anything, it could be said to be pro-cyclical, since its spending ceiling is expressed as a percentage of Community GDP (CEC, 1993d, p. 23). Clearly some additional measure of Community stabilization would be helpful (Italianer and Van Heukelen, 1993). The latter have proposed a reserve to operate outside the general budget which would be transferred in the form of an outright grant to economies suffering an exogenous shock which raised their unemployment rate significantly above the EU average. It would probably account for about 0.22 per cent of EU GDP.

However, one should remember that the EU does undertake loans, especially via the European Investment Bank (EIB); also, the New Community Instrument (Ortoli facility) created in 1978 was conceived as an anti-cyclical weapon, mainly to stimulate investment. In addition, the EIB has been given enhanced powers since the Edinburgh Summit to create the European Investment Fund (EIF) to boost investment. This is injected particularly into TENs and SMEs, including loan guarantees, and also through equity participation.

The degree to which the EU budget can grow in the future depends upon a variety of circumstances and issues. These include the extent to which member states are prepared to see some switch of spending

Table 4.1 Financial perspective for 1993–99 as agreed at the Edinburgh Summit on 12 December 1992 (appropriations for commitments – million ECU, 1992 prices)

	1993	1994	1995	1996	1997	1998	1999
1. CAP	35 230	35 095	35 722	36 364	37 023	37 697	38 389
2. Structural operations	21 277	21 855	23 480	24 990	26 526	28 240	30 000
Structural funds[1]	19 777	20 135	21 480	22 740	24 026	25 690	27 400
Cohesion Funds	1 500	1 750	2 000	2 250	2 500	2 550	2 600
3. Internal policies	3 940	4 084	4 323	4 520	4 710	4 910	5 100
4. External action[2]	3 950	4 000	4 280	4 560	4 830	5 180	5 600
5. Administrative expenditure	3 280	3 380	3 580	3 690	3 800	3 850	3 900
6. Reserves	1 500	1 500	1 100	1 100	1 100	1 100	1 100
Monetary reserve	1 000	1 000	500	500	500	500	500
External loan guarantees	300	300	300	300	300	300	500
Exceptional external expenditure	200	200	300	300	300	300	300
Total commitment appropriations	69 177	69 944	74 485	75 224	77 987	80 977	84 089
Payment appropriations required	65 908	67 036	69 150	71 290	74 491	77 249	80 114
As a % of GNP	1.20	1.19	1.20	1.21	1.23	1.25	1.26
Margin for revision as a % of GNP	0.00	0.01	0.01	0.01	0.01	0.01	0.01
Own resources ceiling as a % of GNP	1.20	1.20	1.21	1.22	1.24	1.26	1.27
1. Objective 1 regions	12 328	13 220	14 300	15 330	16 396	17 820	19 280
2. Total external expenditure including reserves	4 450	4 500	4 880	5 160	5 430	5 780	6 200

Notes:
1. Objective 1 regions
2. Total external expenditure including reserves

Source: CEC (1993d)

upwards to the EU level. For example, unlike other federations which are responsible for defence, the EU, having rejected a European Defence Community in 1954, has operated through NATO. If the United States reduces its defence commitment to western Europe, the EU seems likely to develop via the WEU, and on the basis of Maastricht towards a common foreign policy and defence union. The EU has been unusual in assigning most of its expenditure in a different direction from that of other federations in which defence and social welfare have been so extensive. In contrast, the EU budgetary expenditure has revolved so much (and some would say too much) around agriculture. If the EU is fully to reflect European citizenship in practice, then one could foresee a much bigger transfer of social expenditure towards it, perhaps taking over payment of a minimum EU-wide level of unemployment and social benefits.

In 1977 the MacDougall Report recommended that the EC budget needed to increase to a minimum of 2–2.5 per cent of GDP, and for successful monetary union the budget needed to be raised to 5–7 per cent of EC GDP (CEC, 1977). Whilst the budget could evolve in this under pressure for common defence and social responsibilities, there are also competing elements at work restricting the growth of the EU central budget. These include concerns to decentralize and to operate subsidiarity as enshrined in the Maastricht Treaty. There is also worry about greater waste and lack of democratic accountability in a centralized budget. Many member states are also questioning the traditional role of the state in providing public goods, particularly merit goods. Privatization is reining back the public sector and has spread from Britain to other member states on the grounds of microeconomic efficiency, plus macroeconomic benefits in reducing government borrowing by selling off loss-making state activities and turning round their economic performance.

Unfortunately in my view there has developed too much downgrading of the scope for a larger budget which was recognized in the MacDougall Report. For example, an influential report by an independent group of economists suggests that a small budget of around 2 per cent of GDP could be sufficient to sustain an effective EMU (CEC, 1993d). An increase in the budget to this level is likely to occur where there are common benefits to be reaped by an EU level of provision; for example, the EU role in R&D and in the provision of external assistance to the rest of the world has scope to grow further. EU budgetary expenditure will also rise with enlargement, with a possible doubling of the budget to embrace eastern European countries, including the Visegrad 4 plus the Balkan and Baltic republics and the former republics of the USSR (CEC, 1993d, p. 114).

At the Edinburgh Summit it was necessary to reach agreement on financing and expenditure, since the southern European countries required enhanced structural funds to compensate for and to facilitate their full participation in the SEM. The UK was prepared to accommodate this since it was holding the Council Presidency and wanted a deal, rather than passing on the problem to the next Presidency. The UK was willing to trade off a modest increase in costs if it gained satisfaction on all other issues, such as subsidiarity, an opt-out for Denmark to enable it to approve the Maastricht Treaty, and enlargement to bring in EFTA members (since they would be net contributors to the budget). At the time it appeared that the UK had obtained a satisfactory deal and also retained Mrs Thatcher's Fontainebleau Abatement, equivalent to giving back to the UK two-thirds of the difference between its VAT contribution and receipts. This had given back to the UK £16 billion since Fontainebleau.

When the budget increases agreed at Edinburgh came to be approved by the House of Commons on 28 November 1994, these proved unexpectedly controversial. Despite the Chancellor of the Exchequer's attempts to clarify the position and the rise from 1.20 per cent to 1.27 per cent of GNP by 1999, uncertainty was created about the level of current and future contributions. The net UK budgetary contribution, that is, the difference between its receipts and payments, was estimated to have risen to 2.45 billion pounds. The UK is still the second largest contributor to the budget, behind Germany, yet is in eighth position out of the 12 in living standards. Payments and receipts are shown in Figure 4.1.

Another issue was that since the Edinburgh Summit the UK government had raised domestic taxation and sought to prune national expenditure. Members of Parliament, especially the Eurosceptics, found it hard to stomach increased EU expenditure set against domestic austerity. In particular, 17.5 per cent VAT on fuel was highly unpopular, hitting the poorest hardest. The second stage of the VAT increase inherited by Kenneth Clarke from Norman Lamont was subsequently rejected in the House of Commons, with the Chancellor having to devise a substitute to replace the lost revenue. In the case of EU expenditure, the European Court of Auditors in 1994 produced another report highlighting fraudulent and wasteful expenditure in particular areas,

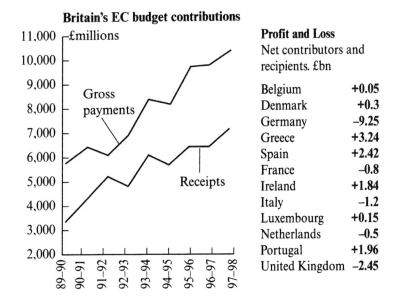

Britain's EC budget contributions

Source: *Sunday Times*, 27 November 1994.

Figure 4.1   Paying the way: EC contributions

especially agriculture. Despite the cutbacks in agricultural price support, particularly export subsidies which are open to abuse and fraud, farmers have been compensated in other ways; also, there are difficulties in containing and reducing agriculture's share of the budget in practice.

The UK government made approval of its EU budgetary arrangements a vote of confidence in itself. Naturally it won, though those MPs who did not support it had the Party Whip removed for a short while and constituted a separate entity from the mainstream Conservative Party. MPs were not satisfied fully by Kenneth Clarke's assurances and letter to them, since budgetary forecasts are unpredictable, depending on rates of economic growth and levels of inflation. The UK's net budgetary contribution is likely to rise to £3.55 billion in 1999, though the EU budget and the UK contribution remain small in relation to national expenditure. However, the divisions in the Conservative Party are likely to constrain the Eurobudget because of concerns about federalism and also the excessive weight of expenditure still devoted to agriculture: the latter is discussed in the following section.

AGRICULTURAL PROBLEMS

Whilst the main focus in this book is on the use of structural funds to help regional development, it is necessary to give a broad account of the CAP and the EAGGF. This is because the latter was set up primarily to finance an agricultural policy rather than a regional policy. Article 39 in the Treaty of Rome only touches upon regional differences in farming structures. Most of the EAGGF expenditure has taken place across the Community and mainly under the guarantee section, with the amount devoted to guidance expenditure failing to reach the level which was first envisaged of around one-third of total expenditure. Statistics for 1992 show that EAGGF guarantee guideline expenditure was ECU 35,039 million (of which total expenditure was ECU 32,108 million). By comparison, guidance section expenditure (commitment appropriations) was ECU 2,875 million. The composition of guarantee spending naturally mainly guarantees prices, but has been modified slightly to include some measures now concerned with structural adjustment, such as set-aside, environmental protection, early retirement, and so on.

The CAP constitutes the most complete EC policy, but has proved contentious and been subject to considerable criticism, particularly by the UK, because of its adverse effects on consumers and its undue dominance of the EC budget. Whilst agriculture now accounts for only a small percentage of EU employment and an even smaller part of EU GDP, it has absorbed about 60 per cent of budgetary expenditure, or some 0.6 per cent of EU GNP. There is also a danger of CAP expenditure running up against the guideline ceiling introduced in 1989. Furthermore, the high budgetary costs of the CAP also underestimate the real income effects to the EU and to the rest of the world. However, the creation and operation of EC agricultural policy have to be put into context. They emerged from and reflect the continuity of continental agricultural policies favouring protectionism and price support policies to ensure sufficient supplies of foodstuffs. Countries worried about continuing post-war shortages and lack of enough foreign exchange naturally succumbed to political pressure for farm support. Farmers were compensated as politicians sought to buy votes and once the CAP was in place there was a continuing vested interest by bureaucrats in presiding over a large expenditure policy. It was also seen as providing the continuing benefits of a traditional rural way of life.

The CAP has been relatively successful in moving from a situation of shortage to surplus and many would view the former as a greater problem than the latter. Also, if one takes a neo-Malthusian view in relation to world overpopulation, or the likelihood of future crop failures, then EC policy might appear prudent. In addition, the adverse effects of nuclear accidents such as that at Chernobyl have shown the potential threats to agricultural supply in localized areas. But even those who believe in purchasing insurance cover to protect against uncertain future events would question the price or the premium which has had to be paid. Also, larger farms have developed which are capable of insuring themselves against substantial reductions in output, both of livestock and arable products. Consequently, though price instability is endemic to agriculture, given the low elasticities, where insurance can be taken out, this weakens the case for stabilizing market prices.

All countries have offered some agricultural support policies, more so as they have become highly developed. Producer Subsidy Equivalent, which is the transfer to producers relative to the value of farm gate output, is 45 per cent in the EU. Generally, agricultural exporting countries have tended to provide the least support (for example, in New Zealand it is as low as 5 per cent), whereas agricultural importing countries have provided the highest level of farm support. The EC, being more densely populated and lacking the comparative advantage in agriculture possessed by North America and Australasia, has preferred protectionism to open free trade in agricultural products. The UK historically is atypical of EU countries because of its early advantage and application of its comparative industrial advantage and the benefits of Empire free trade. Within the EC the UK has had to switch from lower to higher food prices and, in addition, has had to pay again through its disproportionate contribution to the budget which is dominated by the CAP. Other member states brought in through the process of enlargement, being more dependent on agriculture than the UK, have tended to reinforce support for maintaining the essential features of the CAP.

Perhaps the key issue, which even the UK can agree upon, is not so much the case for some agricultural support, but the extent of this, the types of policy which are used, and the financing of these policies. Nowadays the argument has moved on in recognizing the fact that it is not just technical efficiency, but economic efficiency which is most important; that is, to use the factors of production to produce the highest possible level of GDP. It will be shown in this chapter that this is best achieved by reducing market prices and moving towards more direct income support. The CAP will then contribute to economic efficiency, whilst the other valuable aspects of agricultural life can be maintained by a separate rural development policy. These will reflect the positive externalities from a 'green' way of life and a balanced regional distribution of population and employment. Also, policies have been modified to reflect the benefits from agriculture not only in supplying food but in reflecting the environment. The latter was omitted in the original Objectives laid down for the CAP, but subsequent to Article 130 of the Single European Act (SEA) of 1986, environmental protection requirements have been increasingly recognized.

PRINCIPLES, OBJECTIVES AND PRICE SUPPORT

The CAP revolves around three main principles. The first concerns the Single Market, with free unimpeded movement of agricultural products. Secondly, there is a preference for Community farm produce over imported produce, with the latter having to overcome protectionist barriers. Finally, there is financial solidarity in which all share in the costs and benefits of the EAGGF. Obviously, those countries such as the UK with a small agricultural sector would prefer to see different financing, probably involving some re-nationalization of agriculture.

The main objectives of the CAP have been to raise agricultural productivity, thereby ensuring a fair standard of living for the agricultural community; to stabilize markets; to ensure availability of supplies; and to ensure that supplies reach consumers at reasonable prices. These objectives as laid down in Article 39 of the Treaty of Rome were drawn too widely, with a basic conflict between maintaining a fair standard of living for farmers and at the same time providing reasonable prices for consumers. Both of the terms 'fair' and 'reasonable' are subjective. To the extent that consumers observe lower prices for many products on the world market, they conclude that EC prices are unreasonable, even though recognizing that if the EC begins to import more, this will also pull up world market prices. The CAP has certainly been successful in creating more stable prices than those prevailing on world markets. It has also ensured complete security of supplies for most products, with the EC actually being beyond 100 per cent self-sufficiency in many instances. The sternest critics might quibble with the notion of achieving such complete security, also pointing to the continued import of inputs such as fertilizers and the possibly damaging effects which these might create. Scott focuses on long-term insecurity arising in particular from problems of environmental degradation, adverse effects on soil fertility and a narrowing genetic overdependence on a limited range of seed varieties (Scott, 1995, pp. 108–11).

Market price support was introduced by the EC since the original six member states were using this already. Price support ensures that Community farmers receive a stable price and those who cannot dispose of their products on the open market still obtain a minimum price. The latter is brought about by the intervention agencies which are obliged to purchase everything offered, providing the commodity is able to meet quality and quantity criteria. It is mainly in this way that price has been maintained above the equilibrium market level. In addition, more efficient world exporting countries have been prevented from undercutting EC suppliers through the imposition of variable levies to bring the price up to the threshold price. The policy necessitated increasingly ingenious ways of disposing of surplus produce both internally and by the use of export restitutions to enable the EC externally to sell foodstuffs competitively on the world market.

Before moving on in the next section to outline some of the long-overdue reforms to the CAP, it might be noted here (to link up with the later section on structural problems) that the system has tended to benefit the smaller farmers least. It is the 20 per cent of producers with the greatest production which have obtained the lion's share (some 80 per cent of price support), particularly those in northern Europe. They have been the ones best able to fulfil the conditions laid down by the intervention agencies in relation to sufficient quantities of standard products which meet the appropriate quality criteria.

REFORMS WITHOUT RESOLUTION

Fundamental reforms have appeared quite straightforward to economists for years, but have been frustrated by political and social pressures. Economists tend to focus on lowering prices, especially for goods in surplus, and pay more attention to bringing these down towards equilibrium and world market prices. Even though supply is less predictable in response to market signals than most economists might like, it is the price mechanism which is crucial in restoring market equilibrium.

Whilst the EC has come to recognize this, it has only come about very slowly. For example, the Mansholt Plan in 1968 recognized the need to take land out of cultivation, but this was seen as too radical. However, three Directives were introduced in 1972, dealing with farm modernization (though taken up mainly by northern European farmers); cessation of farming and land re-allocation; and supply of guidance and training in new skills. Unfortunately the decade after enlargement in 1973 was largely wasted in terms of reform since the rest of the EC had access to the large UK import market. The costs of the CAP soared and during the 1980s overproduction increased. The EC, despite cutting prices in real terms, found that world prices had fallen even more. Instead the EC preferred to skirt around lowering prices sufficiently by resorting to other piecemeal measures of control, such as quotas, but these only affect supply, whereas lowering prices reduces supply and stimulates demand. Quotas have been used to control, for example, sugar beet and milk output.

Policies to squeeze prices have had to be pursued more fully, limiting purchases to a guaranteed threshold, below which target and intervention prices have been reduced. Also, producers have had to participate in the disposing of their surpluses through co-responsibility levies, such as for milk and cereals, to cover policy operating costs. There have also been attempts to stimulate consumption through consumer subsidies and marketing campaigns. In addition there was some attempt to diversify products such as switching from milk to beef production and using oil seed production to substitute partly for cereals. EC policy in recent years has recognized the need to introduce additional controls through input quotas. One example of this is set-aside, in which farmers are paid to take land out of cultivation and act in practice as environmental park-keepers. Set-aside has been used for many years in the United States with limited effects. Although output falls, this is not in direct proportion to the land set aside, since farmers set aside the poorest and most marginal land and farm their existing land more intensively. Also, after land has been fallow, fertility is increased when it is returned to production by rotation.

EC policy of lowering farm prices, imposing output and input quotas, and placing a ceiling on the CAP's share of the EC budget are all steps in the right direction. There is also some evidence of policy success in reducing overproduction in particular sectors. Beef intervention stocks are down; butter stocks peaked in 1986 and have fallen back. Stocks of grain, which were over 30 million tonnes in 1992, fell to about 25 million tonnes at the end of 1993. Cereal production has fallen, partly because of set-aside. However, the Court of Auditors has shown that agricultural fraud has continued to raise costs; for example, wine production has risen by one-fifth since 1989, in spite of EU spending of ECU 2 billion to take vineyards out of production. Also, EU payments to persuade wine and milk producers to cut production are still being offset by policy incentives to raise output.

The case for reform in the 1990s mounted further as a result of the interaction of internal and external pressures. Enlargement of the EU, with its growing costs, has led to fears that further enlargement to include eastern Europe could prove overwhelming in terms of additional budgetary costs. In 1995 the EU was hopeful that enlargement to include the three EFTA countries (Austria, Finland and Sweden) would mean that they would have to adapt to even lower prices, thus creating some potential for imports into the EFTA markets from the rest of the EU and the rest of the world. It is pressure from the latter which ultimately convinced the EU that reform was inevitable and would be easier if all partners adjusted, since there were gains to be reaped in other traded sectors. The USA was insistent in the Uruguay Round that agriculture should not continue to be excluded as in previous GATT negotiations. The USA was joined in its determination to reduce the level of agricultural support by the Cairns Group, which includes Australia and New Zealand.

Reform of the CAP developed to enable EU agricultural policy to accommodate the GATT settlement. The main feature of CAP reform is a 30 per cent cut in cereal prices from mid 1993 to mid 1996. Cereal prices are to fall to ECU 110 per tonne, though this fall is still less than the Commission had wanted. The intervention price will be 10 per cent lower at ECU 100 per tonne, but a very high threshold price is retained at ECU 155 per tonne (whereas the Commission proposed that the threshold price should be only 10 per cent above the target price). This will result in cheaper feedstocks, helping to bring down prices in other sectors. Since permanent compensatory aids are integral to offset negative income effects, cereal farmers are to be fully compensated on average. Farmers receive compensation per hectare equal to the price reduction multiplied by the average regional yield. Eligibility for compensation for all except the smallest cereal farms (less than 92 tonnes production) is based on setting aside 15 per cent of their land, for which they will also be given compensation. Whilst this is likely to continue to reduce the rate of growth of production, it may not be sufficient to resolve the overproduction problem. The most efficient cereal farmers will still find it profitable to increase production at the lower prices. This has been reinforced by suspension of cereal co-responsibility levies (Scott, 1995, p. 116).

Apart from the major reform of the cereal sector, milk quotas are being cut by 1 per cent per annum over the three years from 1993/4, and butter intervention prices were reduced by 2.5 per cent per annum for 1993/4 and 1994/5. The dairy sector changes are far less than those envisaged in the original MacSharry proposals. Milk production, despite a quota, has been relatively unaffected by the recent reforms. However, there has been a significant cut of 15 per cent in beef price support, and beef cattle, along with sheep, are to be subject to quotas. The various measures are to be implemented through member state programmes, with normally half of the cost being borne from the CAP budget, but with 75 per cent of the cost being met by the EU for Objective 1 regions. Farmers are to be compensated for early retirement.

A GATT agreement was reached despite French reservations, since the EU recognized that failure to settle would be even more unfortunate because of its adverse impact on other traded sectors. It has been agreed that internal agricultural support will be reduced by 20 per cent over the six years from 1995. This Aggregate Measure of Support sums the value of all direct/indirect farm support, excluding any non-trade distorting elements. One of the most significant changes introduced is that of tariffication: that is, the conversion of all import barriers, particularly levies, into a fixed tariff as the only measure of protection. These tariffs are then to be reduced on average by 36 per cent over the six years from 1995. Countries also have to offer a reduced import tariff for each agricultural product subject to the tariffs on a quantity eventually equal to 5 per cent of domestic consumption. Export subsidies, which existed on a large scale as the EC competitively dumped its agricultural products on the world market, are to be reduced by 36 per cent over the six years from 1995 from their 1986–90 levels. The volume of subsidized exports has to contract by 21 per cent over the same period. It is a welcome recognition that the dumping of agricultural products is as damaging to efficient producers as the dumping of industrial products. Since the EC has always recognized the latter, though from the viewpoint mainly of an importer, logic dictates that it should equally accept the same for agricultural products.

The purpose of these reforms is to cut the growth of agricultural yields in the EC from 2 per cent to 1 per cent per annum. If it fails to depress yields sufficiently and these increase at 1.5 per cent per annum, then a further twist will be necessary to the policies outlined, such as necessitating setting aside 30 per cent of land. What has made the policy generally acceptable is that decoupling, whereby price support is severely pruned, has been accompanied by offsetting income support. Since the latter is more transparent it will be subject to even greater political pressure to constrain agricultural expenditure in future.

Environmental measures, though less than 1 per cent of CAP expenditure over the next five years, also reflect a step in the right direction; for example, to reduce the amount of intensive farming by restricting the use of fertilizers and encouraging more organic farming. Finance is also available for environmental protection of farmland, woodland and managing the land for alternative uses. Ultimately, however, the EU is in a dilemma whereby it is criticized for excessive expenditure in paying many farmers to produce unwanted food, and now is moving towards paying farmers to produce no food but to carry out a park-keeping role.

Further reforms will be needed in the future to reduce the costs of the CAP which otherwise will escalate; significantly if east European enlargement takes place. Although currently most east European countries are net importers of foodstuffs, dynamically their potential to raise farm output would be considerably increased unless EU prices continue to be brought down closer towards world market levels. The MacSharry package and GATT settlement covers only about half of EC agricultural output. Whilst the adoption of direct payments to farmers is welcome, these are not completely decoupled from output, nor are they targeted sufficiently to farmers in need. Deeper price-cuts will be necessary, though probably resisted after the major reforms now undertaken. These reforms might include, after a limited time period up to the year 2000, a phased switching of most EU farm subsidies into national budgets and compensating member states through the regional, social and Cohesion Funds. In addition, alternative re-allocations of agricultural spending may be sought based on modified criteria, for example, the environmental criterion of using either agricultural land area or total land area (which would include forest, mountainous areas and urban land). An alternative rural approach might allocate expenditure using a criterion in proportion to either employment in agriculture or total rural population. The effects of these changes are shown in Table 4.2, favouring poorer southern European countries by reducing expenditure in general in northern Europe.

Table 4.2   Alternative allocations of agricultural budget, 1986–88

	Environmental (per capita of national population, EC = 100)			Rural development	
	1986–88 actual	agric.	all land	empl.	popn.
Denmark	293	154	122	78	65
Germany	94	53	57	48	65
Netherlands	266	10	10	56	56
Belgium	114	39	45	37	14
UK	45	83	62	33	37
France	139	142	140	94	121
Italy	88	77	76	132	149
Ireland	415	396	140	258	196
Spain	32	108	187	148	107
Portugal	15	96	62	358	317
Greece	182	53	190	302	177
EC(12) (average)	100	100	100	100	100

Notes:
*EAGGF Budget
Environmental allocations in proportion to:
agric. – agricultural land area.
all land – total land area.
Rural development allocations in proportion to:
empl. – full-time equivalent persons engaged in agriculture.
popn. – total population in rural area.

Source: S. Holland (1993).

STRUCTURAL PROBLEMS

Agricultural employment has declined in the member states of the EU. Statistics on agricultural employment vary, with the principal sources being the Labour Force Survey, which is an annual survey of about 1 per cent of households in the EU. It is the source for comparing agriculture with other sectors. Family workers are not distinguished in the UK. Another source is the Farm Structure Survey which is a two yearly sample survey of agricultural holdings and relates the holder to the holding. The Agricultural Labour Force comprises the holder, family workers and non-family labour. Agricultural employment in the EU has fallen at an average rate of 2.8 per cent per annum since 1960. By the early 1990s about 9 million people worked the equivalent of a full year in agriculture, but nearly 18 million are still attached to the land in some way. The employment of part-time workers means that in addition to the Agricultural Labour Force a different measure is also used, called the Annual Work Unit (AWU). This relates to the amount of agricultural work done by a full-time employee, which is estimated at 2 200 hours per annum. Since many agricultural workers are part-time, employment is usually expressed by the AWU rather than the numbers employed.

Whilst a continued reduction in agricultural employment and the reduction of disguised unemployment in that sector is to be welcomed in raising productivity, it has given rise to particular problems. For example, it has left an ageing farm population, even more elderly when farmers rather than the agricultural workers are examined. Half of all farmers are over 55 years of age. Also, these elderly farmers are concentrated on very small holdings, especially in southern Europe. Further contraction of agriculture will lead to a cutback of many agricultural facilities in rural areas.

Agricultural incomes vary significantly, being lower on the farms which are smaller and with a poorer structure, particularly in southern Europe. Furthermore, dual job-holding is more characteristic of the richer northern agricultural areas, such as Germany, because of higher overall demand. In southern Europe, despite an increased worker supply incentive to take two jobs, there is less opportunity to take alternative work, hence the existence of significant underemployment and lower incomes in southern Europe. The European Size Unit (ESU) is the agricultural definition used to reflect the economic income-generating capacity of a holding, as opposed to the physical size of the holding. One ESU was equal to ECU 1 200 (in 1991) of Standard Gross Margin (the difference between the value of gross agricultural production minus the specific input costs of that production).

There is a wide variation in yields and incomes, and further divergence between agricultural regions seems likely as the larger farmers benefit from economies of scale. The main constraint on such divergence is provided by increased pollution adversely affecting the environment; for example, high livestock densities creating excess manure, and so on. In addition, larger farms are better suited to supplying the quantities and high quality demanded by the growth of large supermarkets.

STRUCTURAL POLICY

EAGGF guidance expenditure provides aid to Objective 1 regions which are lagging behind in development; to Objective 5a for agricultural structure in all regions, with no territorial limitations; and to Objective 5b, which concerns rural areas with certain limitations. These have a low level of economic development and also need to satisfy two out of three of the following conditions for eligibility: high agricultural unemployment; low agricultural incomes; low population density and/or a significant depopulation trend. These also now include, under the re-

Table 4.3   Expenditure trend by Objective, 1988–92 (million ECU)

Objective	1988	1989	1990	1991	1992
Objective 1 (regions lagging behind)	555.223[2]	862.129	1 081.157	1 440.827	1 634.683
Objective 5a (agricultural structures)		516.204	743.811	631.252	701.333
Objective 5b (development of rural measures)	624.778	26.856	44.005	260.152	475.798
Transitional measures[1]		56.802	56.703	75.928	63.000
TOTAL	1 180.000	1 461.991	1 925.676	2 408.159	2 874.814

Notes:
[1]   Expenditure under old measures that cannot be assigned to any of the present Objectives.
[2]   Estimate based on regional expenditure statistics.

Source: CEC (1994c).

vised regulations, restructuring of the fisheries sector. The distribution of expenditure under the three Objectives is shown in Table 4.3. Expenditure on Objective 1 has grown rapidly as a result of the concentration of the structural funds in these regions and was three times higher in 1992 than in 1988.

Rural development consists of horizontal measures to help all farmers who need assistance. These cover production (for example, increasing competitiveness, diversification into non-farming activities, and so on), processing and marketing products. In the Objective 1 regions the guidance section finances entirely horizontal measures which under Objective 5a are integrated in the financing plan for the CSFs. It also part-finances, with the ERDF and ESF, regionalized measures which correspond to the specific needs of each region. This is shown in Table 4.4.

In most of the programmes the measures relate to improvements in rural infrastructure, crop conversion, improving production conditions, environmental protection and reafforestation. The latter has often consisted of overplanting of fast-growing trees such as conifers and eucalyptus.

Under Objective 5b in rural areas outside Objective 1 regions, spending concentrates on five broad priorities: diversification of the primary

Table 4.4   Single fund and multi-fund operational programmes in the Objective 1 regions with an EAGGF input, 1989–93 (million ECU at current prices)

Member state	Regionalized measures	Horizontal measures	EAGGF total
Greece	676	763	1 439
Spain	800	624	1 424
France	150	52	202
Ireland	247	489	736
Italy	540	335	875
Portugal	652	633	1 285
United Kingdom (Northern Ireland)	52	90	142
Total	3 117	2 986	6 103

Source: CEC (1994c).

sector; development of non-agricultural sectors; conservation and development of the natural environment; development of human resources; and the fostering of tourism. The Commission has encouraged the adoption of integrated programmes, and more than 70 per cent of these under Objective 5b are multi-funded between EAGGF guidance spending plus the ERDF and ESF (see Table 4.5).

Table 4.5 Community funding of Objective 5b, 1989–93 (Breakdown by member state and by fund, in round figures, in millions ECU at 1989 prices)

Member state	EAGGF Guidance section	ERDF	ESF	Total
Belgium	11.0	11.3	9.7	32.5
Denmark	4.5	12.2	6.3	23.0
Germany	194.4	235.5	95.1	525.0
Spain	184.9	61.1	39.0	285.0
France	449.0	335.0	176.0	960.0
Italy	184.9	145.4	54.7	385.0
Luxembourg	1.42	0.9	0.18	2.5
Netherlands	12.5	24.9	6.6	44.0
United Kingdom	24.9	276.8	48.3	350.0
EC total	1 068	1 103	436	2 607

Source: CEC (1994c).

Many operations have been financed by the LEADER (a French acronym for 'Links between Actions for the Development of the Rural Economy'). Funds have been dispersed to local bodies, mainly to implement innovatory projects for rural development. For example, it employs people to go into agricultural villages to talk to residents and conceive ideas. These projects are wide-ranging, from environmental improvements to tele-cottages, and are then owned by local people, often as co-operatives. Much of the labour is by unpaid volunteers. It is therefore a desirable example of encouraging grass roots development, though it has been criticized as being separate from and not integrated into the CSFs.

In addition, there is specific aid for those farmers operating in less favoured and marginal areas, such as mountainous regions and hill farming areas in particular. This change was introduced in 1975 and was a welcome step forward. In areas of high altitude with poor weather conditions and steep slopes, compensation is necessary to maintain activity. The farmer in turn agrees to continue operating there for a period of five years after the first payment. It is necessary to maintain some rural population in such areas. These less favoured areas now total 55 per cent of all the utilized agricultural areas in the EU (CEC, 1994c). Note that the Utilized Agricultural Area refers to the amount of land used for agricultural purposes and usually excludes forestry and fish farming.

Rural strategies are different for those rural areas which are in close proximity to urban areas where part-time industrial and service work is possible and in which the rural environment provides natural opportunities for leisure and recreation for city dwellers. In contrast, developing the outlying peripheral and underdeveloped agricultural areas which are in decline, especially in southern Europe and Ireland, necessitates agricultural restructuring and the development of new industrial and service activity. In Ireland, alternative employment has been provided by encouraging inward investment in a generally satisfactory way, though without developing sufficient links within the local economy. From an environmental angle it is necessary to encourage non-polluting firms, promote recycling and provide special incentives to SMEs, especially where new technology is involved. There is a need to encourage strategies which focus particularly on local resources.

To alleviate the problems caused by the decline of agriculture, tourism has offered a useful means of development. It is the biggest sector in the EU, though it was not until 1980 that an embryonic EU tourism policy began to emerge, with a Commissioner being given specific responsibility for tourism. In 1985 a small tourism sector was created in the Transport Directorate (DG VII) which in 1989 was transferred to a new DG XXIII for Enterprise, Tourism and Social Economy. The year 1990 was designated European Year of Tourism, followed in 1991 by a focus mainly on rural-cultural tourism. Tourism requires investment in both transport infrastructure and accommodation. Marketing a range of mixed and linked attractions within the region is important. This can then be followed by the creation of transnational links between EU regions which have a common product to market. There is a myriad of examples ranging from cycle and horse-drawn carriage trails across borders, to cross-border fishing and routes for European wine and beer enthusiasts.

The use of tourism to promote the sale of local products is important. Just one example is that of the Syndicat d'Aménagement des Baronnies in France, selling fresh herbs such as lavender, thyme and tarragon, and goats' cheese, and so on, on local farms. Les Baronnies is a sparsely populated area in south-eastern France, heavily dependent on agriculture with its traditional products such as olive oil, lavender and aromatic oils. It has tried to tackle its local problems through the Syndicat which has brought together those concerned with agricultural improvements and the promotion of tourism through the sale of local products. It has been argued that other rural areas in the EU could benefit from further study of Les Baronnies' experience. Another interesting but different example of tourist development is a women's Agrotourism Co-operative at Petra, Mytillini Island, Greece. The women have provided bed and breakfast, but have also come together to engage in additional joint activities to promote tourism.

It can be seen that there is now less emphasis on agricultural support policy *per se* and instead a focus on regional rural development programmes. The aim is to broaden the base of activities in rural areas and to diversify the pattern of production. This involves a more diversified agricultural structure, also exploiting new agricultural opportunities, such as recycling agricultural waste in an environmentally friendly manner. Agriculture is in addition being increasingly associated and linked to tourism, often with the sale of local products. Through infrastructure improvement and proactive flexible support to SMEs, new industries and service activities are beginning to develop; these are conducive to stabilizing and offsetting the natural decline of employment in agricultural activities. Rural policies depend increasingly upon endogenous development, with strong emphasis upon local community involvement harnessed through a spirit of partnership. The EU has information centres, especially in Objective 1 and Objective 5b regions, to provide advice and to encourage rural development.

THE COMMON FISHERIES POLICY (CFP) AND THE FINANCIAL INSTRUMENT FOR FISHERIES GUIDANCE (FIFG)

It is important to consider fisheries since the Treaty of Rome included these in its definition of agricultural products; also, a separate fisheries policy (the CFP) is in operation. This was conceived shortly before the first enlargement of the EC, which took place in 1973, and was an attempt to cover the fishing industry before much more significant fishing nations joined the EC. In fact, this has been one factor leading to Norwegian rejection of membership on two occasions. There are some similarities between the CAP and the CFP, such as market price support, quotas and structural measures. Not only the CAP but also the CFP has been difficult to operate effectively and comes in for major criticism. The UK feels particularly aggrieved about both policies, with the principle of equal access making significant inroads into the national fish catch. Iberian enlargement and the high consumption of fish per head in Spain and Portugal (which is sustained by large fishing fleets) have led to continuing conflicts with other member states, such as the UK. The upshot is that whereas the CAP has led to agricultural surpluses, the CFP and overfishing (in spite of conservation measures) have led to a growing shortage of particular fish species. With massive overcapacity of vessels in the fishing industry, structural measures have been needed and these are now consolidated by a new FIFG as a part of the structural funds.

Turning to the particular problems emanating from the decline of the fishing industry, the task of dealing with these has been given to the FIFG. The measures to be undertaken include contributing to achieving a sustainable balance between resources and their exploitation; strengthening the competitiveness of structures and the development of economically viable enterprises; and improving market supply and the value added to fisheries and aquaculture products. Assistance may be given to measures concerned with redeployment operations, joint ventures and adjustment of capacities. Investments and operations covered relate to fields such as the following: restructuring and renewal of the fishing fleet; modernization of the fishing fleet; improvement of the conditions under which fishery and aquaculture products are processed and marketed; development of aquaculture and structural works in coastal waters; exploratory fishing; facilities at fishing ports; search for new markets; and specific measures (see Council Regulation No. 2080/93).

5. Evolution of regional policies: the ERDF and structural fund reforms

OUTLINE

The creation of the ECSC and the EEC was dominated by the principle of free market competition. However, the Treaty of Rome (1957) led to the establishment of bodies such as the EAGGF, the ESF and the EIB which were to play a major role in regional policy. The latter was needed mainly because of the severe regional imbalance experienced in the south of Italy *vis-à-vis* the rest of the EC. During the 1950s and 1960s overall unemployment remained low and the Commission Directorate of Competition favoured competition policies, but there were provisions for the weakest regions to be given special assistance. This chapter begins by highlighting regional policy in the original six member states, followed by an examination of the particular role of the EIB in supporting the operation of the structural funds. It then covers the development of a common regional policy stimulated by enlargement of the Community. It concentrates particularly upon the operation of the ERDF, its objectives, the revised regulations and reforms.

REGIONAL POLICY FOR THE ORIGINAL SIX MEMBER STATES

When the ECSC was set up in 1951 under the Treaty of Paris to cover these strategic sectors, no big contraction in demand for coal and steel products was foreseen. However, the Treaty did recognize a need to safeguard continuity of employment and it permitted compensation of workers who were made redundant. Given the heavily localized nature of coal and steel production, contraction proved to be a major source of disturbance in the areas affected. During the 1960s the coal industry declined with the switch to cheaper sources of energy, particularly oil. Whereas coal accounted for nearly two-thirds of primary energy consumption in 1960, by 1985 this had fallen to under a quarter. A nationalized coal industry can afford to adopt an average cost pricing policy to break even, but the move towards more commercial criteria leads to the closure of marginal pits.

The steel industry underwent a longer period of economic expansion than coal, and since the early 1970s has suffered cutbacks, restructuring and heavy unemployment. Traditional steel-making areas which operated old-fashioned, small-scale plants and which were in close proximity to local sources of ore have been closed down. New giant plants have been constructed increasingly at coastal sites using imported ore and benefiting from the huge economies of scale in the industry.

The ECSC, unlike the EEC, has been involved in housing by offering loans at minimal interest rates to improve living conditions of workers by the construction, purchase or modernization of housing. Also, the High Authority of the ECSC has provided assistance for readaptation of labour, helping with retraining, resettlement and compensation. It generally contributed up to 50 per cent of the costs involved. Assistance with industrial reconversion did not occur until the late 1950s when it was clear that readaptation of the workforce was insufficient. It then provided temporary subsidies and help with new investment and in attracting new enterprise through site improvement. Expenditure on reconversion soon exceeded that on readaptation of labour and during the 1980s the Davignon Plan required further expenditure to restructure and slim down the steel industry to increase its competitive efficiency.

The Treaty of Rome, in the economic buoyancy of the 1950s, likewise contained no specific provisions to create a common regional policy. There were mainly exceptions provided on regional grounds to modify the operation of sectoral EC policies in fields such as agriculture and transport. The prevailing emphasis was on a strong competition policy which sought to root out the multitude of state aids which would distort free competition, but some derogation was permissible on regional grounds.

During the 1960s the EC commissioned various studies of regional problems and made some progress in categorizing different types of problem regions. The Commission then made clear the policies it favoured for different regions; for example, in underdeveloped regions it placed emphasis on infrastructure, and it also focused on growth poles based on a study of the Bari–Brindisi–Taranto growth pole in the heel of the Mezzogiorno. For old industrial regions the Commission emphasized measures such as attracting new industries and retraining labour. However, the EC failed to establish the statistical criteria to be used in determining the magnitude of the problem and which areas precisely would be helped.

The EC was mainly concerned up to 1969 with controlling national aids. It then conceived the potential for pursuing a more active role for itself. This was reflected in its Memorandum on Regional Policy which in 1969 suggested the establishment of a Regional Development Rebate Fund to provide a rebate on interest payments. However, this did not materialize and instead the EC continued to focus mainly on controlling and co-ordinating national regional policies. It was considered necessary to prevent member states outbidding each other by over-generous assistance to areas, some of which did not need such help. Since the aim of the EC is to have free and fair competition, it insisted after 1971 in its first resolution on general aid schemes that these were not to exceed 20 per cent of the cash value of investment in the central or so-called 'prosperous areas'. All aid given should also be transparent, that is, open and precisely calculable, thereby ruling out special investment allowances against tax, since future profits were not known. In addition, the aids were to be directed to regions rather than to whole countries (apart from Luxembourg). They were to be graduated and determined according to the severity of the regional problem.

Meanwhile, the EC operated its expenditure policies consciously to alleviate regional problems. This is illustrated in the next section by the functioning of the EIB.

THE EIB

The EIB is bigger than the World Bank in its borrowing and lending, though is more reactive and less proactive than the latter. Although new international banking organizations (such as the European Bank for Reconstruction and Development) have been established to stimulate the development of a market economy in eastern Europe in the 1990s, the EIB is complementary to this. The EIB provides some of its capital, and with its experience and track record is often involved in co-financing projects. The EIB has a much wider geographical spread of lending, though the bulk of it is confined within the EU.

The EIB has a Triple A rating, which is more than can be said for all member states. Its financial stability has been achieved partly by not taking huge risks, leading some to see the EIB as being insufficiently risk-taking or flexible, and also aloof. However, recently the risks of lending have grown with the rise of the private sector, to some extent replacing the governmental sector and increasing lending to the riskier outside world. Hence the Bank took the precautionary measure for the first time in 1992 of making a general provision for bad debts of ECU 150 million in its balance sheet.

The Bank is an independent, non-profit-making institution which lends on a long-term basis. These loans take the form of 8–12 years for industrial projects and 10–20 years or longer for infrastructure. They are usually fixed rate, but can be revisable or variable. Also, there may be a period of grace for repayment, normally of 3–5 years. Loans are linked to the EIB's own borrowing costs, plus a margin of 0.15 per cent to cover its operating costs.

Borrowing

The EIB raises money on international money markets to finance its investments. Money is obtained in appropriate currencies, and the Bank pioneered the use of the ECU. The Bank leaves it mainly to the borrower to choose the currency in which it wants the loan. Some 15 years ago about half of EIB borrowings were raised on non-EC markets. In the 1990s, most of its resources have been raised on EC markets since its customers wanted to borrow in these currencies. The Bank has made increasing use of large-scale issues (Jumbos). It has also stimulated the development of capital markets in various Community countries, helping to kick-start some of them (*EIB Information*, No. 68, June 1991).

Lending

Whilst the EIB has to borrow in order to lend, it is the impact of the latter which is of particular interest. It is relevant in terms of its increasing level and its composition between different sectors within the EU, and between the EU and the rest of the world. The Bank conducts a comprehensive financial, economic, engineering and environmental appraisal to ensure that the projects financed are sufficiently robust. Since the Bank is carrying out EU policy, such as projects of Community interest, its closest links are with the Commission and the various DGs, such as DG XVI for Regional Policy, and the various DGs concerned with external relations and development when lending outside the EU.

Table 5.1   Geographical breakdown of loans granted by the EU,
1993

	ECU million	of which Edinburgh	%	%
Within the European Community	**17 724.2**	**2 363.3**	**100**	
Belgium	371.6	*151.3*	2.1	
Denmark	875.5	*188.0*	4.9	
Germany	2 096.6¹	*287.8*	11.8	
Greece	511.1	*86.5*	2.9	
Spain	4 005.1	*344.4*	22.6	
France	2 205.5	*300.0*	12.4	
Ireland	388.2	*49.7*	2.2	90.4
Italy	3 362.0	*446.1*	19.0	
Luxembourg	–	–	–	
Netherlands	379.7	*23.3*	2.1	
Portugal	1 488.8	*186.2*	8.4	
United Kingdom	1 929.1	*300.0*	10.9	
Other²	111.0		0.6	
Outside the European Community	**1 887.2**		**100.0**	
ACP states	225.7		12.0	
of which 'risk capital'	78.3			
Mediterranean countries	680.5		36.1	9.6
of which 'risk capital'	1.5			
Central and eastern Europe	882.0		46.7	
Asia/Latin America	99.0		5.2	
Grand total	**19 611.4**			**100**

Notes:
1   Including a guarantee for ECU 51.5 million.
2   Projects located outside the member states but, because of their benefit to the EC treated as equivalent to investment within the Community.

Source: EIB Information, February 1994, no. 79.

The total EIB lending limit is up to two-and-a-half times its subscribed capital; that is, lending up to ECU 144 billion. By the end of 1992 its cumulative lending was less than 60 per cent of this statutory ceiling. In the year 1993 the EIB lent ECU 19.6 billion (including ECU 2.4 billion under the Edinburgh lending facility). ECU 17.7 billion was within the EU and ECU 1.9 billion was lent outside the Community. The distribution of this lending is shown in Table 5.1 between the 12 member states and also for those areas outside.

The EIB funds on average about 30 per cent of total project cost. Overall the total investments which it has financed have been estimated at over 5 per cent of Gross Fixed Capital Formation (GFCF). Also, there is a much higher percentage of GFCF in poorer member states: 22 per cent in Portugal, 15 per cent in Greece, and 14 per cent in Spain and Ireland (*EIB Information*, No. 79, February 1994).

Total lending is obviously a function of the willingness of borrowers to invest. Given the slowdown in economic growth during the recession in the 1990s, this has led to the EU taking special measures. These emerged from the European Council Meeting at Edinburgh in December 1992 which introduced two new financing measures to stimulate economic recovery. The first of these was a temporary lending facility of ECU 5 billion, particularly to finance capital infrastructure projects, notably connected with the TENs. Since the Copenhagen and Brussels European Councils in 1993, the duration of the Edinburgh lending facilities has been extended beyond 1994 and also increased from ECU 5 billion to ECU 8 billion. The additional ECU 3 billion is to be composed of ECU 2 billion for TENs and ECU 1 billion for SMEs. The ceiling for these has been raised from 50 per cent to 75 per cent of the investment's costs. The combined ceiling of EIB loans and EU grants was also raised from 70 per cent to 90 per cent.

The second new financing measure was the establishment of the new EIF. This was to be legally independent, to have a capital of ECU 2 billion, subscribed by the EIB (40 per cent), the EC (30 per cent), and public and private banks (30 per cent). The EIF is located at the EIB headquarters in Luxembourg and managed there. It issues guarantees for loans on infrastructure, especially TENs and SMEs. At a later stage it may provide equity participation for both TENs and SMEs (*EIB Information*, No. 76, May 1993). There is an interest rate subsidy for SMEs which is linked to the creation of jobs. This emphasis on SMEs has become increasingly necessary because economic uncertainty has reduced even further the willingness to take risks during the recession.

The composition of EIB lending is in line with its support of European goals. Historically, about two-thirds of its lending has been prioritized for regional development. From 1989–93 EIB financing for regional development amounted to ECU 47 billion and in 1993 this reached 74 per cent of its total lending. Its regional expenditure has been concentrated in those areas eligible for assistance from the structural funds. Ninety per cent of its assistance has gone to these areas, with 58 per cent to Objective 1 regions and 32 per cent to Objective 2 and Objective 5b regions. The Bank also started to lend more to the eastern *Länder* in Germany during these years, whereas before only a few regions in the old *Bundesländer* were classified under EC regional policy. The Bank is increasingly at the forefront in implementing Community policies; for example, the Maastricht Treaty enhances the co-operation and co-ordination between the EIB and the structural funds and the new Cohesion Fund. The Bank not only appraises investments which are co-financed, but may appraise projects where it is not itself a lender but is appraising on behalf of the structural funds. The EIB is also involved in the Integrated Mediterranean Programmes (IMPs), plus support for other EU programmes, such as Envireg, Interreg, and so on.

The EIB was clearly more significant as the sole general source of funding for regional development before the creation of the ERDF. Also, since the SEA of July 1987, designed to bolster economic and social cohesion, regional policy was enhanced further by doubling the structural funds by 1993. However, the EIB's role is a complementary one of supplying loans to reinforce the grants from the structural funds. The EIB is mainly concerned with Objective 1, Objective 2 and, to a lesser extent, Objective 5b areas. The CSFs, which are the response to the national plans submitted by member states, are monitored and assessed by all parties. These consist of the Commission and the member state concerned, along with the EIB. The latter is also represented in a non-voting capacity on the committees of each of the funds. The EIB in its financing and partnership with the structural funds is generally limited to 50 per cent of total investment costs. The Bank ensures that cumulative assistance in the forms of loans and grants does not usually exceed 70 per cent of aggregate costs, although in exceptional cases it could reach 90 per cent.

The role of the EIB goes well beyond regional development (which is the main concern of this book) to balanced EU development in general. It finances particular projects, providing communications infrastructure, conserving the environment and quality of life, boosting the competitive base industrially, helping SMEs and supporting EU energy policy. The latter has become particularly important since the oil price hike in the 1970s, showing the acute vulnerability of the EU with its overdependence on unstable imported supplies.

Finally, let us turn briefly to the EIB's increasing demand to finance projects outside its borders. It has been agreed that normally lending outside the EU will be no more than 10 per cent. EU lending, which was concentrated at first mainly on the African, Caribbean and Pacific countries (ACP) through the Lomé Conventions, has been broadened to embrace other parts of the world, such as southern Europe, eastern Europe and Latin America. For example, lending to eastern Europe and the Mediterranean areas is now far above that to the ACP. This is shown in Table 5.1 on the geographical breakdown of loans granted in 1993. EIB lending to central and eastern Europe began in 1990. The Bank is now spread very widely and having to engage in difficult and more risky analysis. It advances loans to all of these external borrowers from its own resources for economically viable projects, usually offering an interest rate subsidy. Moreover, under mandate from member states or the Community, the Bank administers risk capital offering more flexible repayment formulae.

REGIONAL POLICY AFTER THE FIRST ENLARGEMENT

EC regional policy really took off positively after 1973, mainly as a result of enlargement to nine members, with the recognition of particularly severe regional problems in the UK and Ireland. For example, the Thomson Report on the Regional Problems of the Enlarged Community (CEC, 1973) produced statistics on income per head, unemployment and net emigration. These showed that UK GNP had fallen to 97 per cent of the EC average of 100 by 1970. Using personal income figures, UK regions varied between 73 per cent of EC average in Northern Ireland and 94 per cent in south-east England. Irish regions were far lower on personal incomes, ranging from 41 per cent in the west of Ireland to 65 per cent in the east.

Apart from regional problems *per se*, it was recognized that a regional policy could help to offset the budgetary imbalance which was experienced by the UK after joining the EC. In addition, the pressure for continued integration in other fields, such as the Werner Report in 1970 advocating EMU, reinforced the need to strengthen regional policy to offset the loss of other policy instruments such as exchange rate depreciation (Coffey, 1995).

After two years' negotiation the ERDF was created in 1975, though the size of the fund was restricted because of German reservations. From the viewpoint of recipients, this was unfortunate since the need for regional assistance increased during the 1970s because of recession and rising unemployment following the oil price increases.

Apart from its limited resources, there were two major criticisms. First, there was not enough concentration of spending on the most disadvantaged countries. Richer countries were also obtaining funding to deal with their regional problems. Over the ten year period before Iberian enlargement, some 22 per cent of ERDF spending occurred in countries which had a GDP per capita above the EC average (Wise and Gibb, 1993, p. 217). Secondly, the financing mechanism was mainly under national control; that is, ERDF funding was for projects which were submitted by member states (Keating and Jones, 1985).

It was partly to tackle this high degree of national control that a non-quota section of the ERDF was introduced which would be controlled by the EC. From 1978–80 this was set at only 5 per cent of total ERDF expenditure. Also, every project in it had to be subjected to the unanimous approval of ministers, thus helping to retain member state control. The takeup of the small quota fund was disappointing, since member states were reluctant to submit their proposals to Community scrutiny and questioning. As a result, part of the small quota element remained unspent and was transferred back to the national quota. The Commission, pushing for greater control itself, proposed that there should be an increase in the non-quota section of up to 20 per cent of the total.

POST-1985: THE MOVE TO PROGRAMMES

The distinction between quota and non-quota expenditure was replaced by flexible quota guidelines. The lower limit set the minimum which a member state was entitled to receive and the upper limit was the maximum it could attain. The total minimum expenditure was fixed at 88.63 per cent of the ERDF expenditure, enabling the Commission to exercise discretion over how the remaining 11.37 per cent was spent. Obvi-

Table 5.2   ERDF national shares: 1986 percentages

Country	Lower limit	Upper limit
Italy	21.62	28.79
Spain	17.97	23.93
United Kingdom	14.50	19.31
Portugal	10.66	14.20
Greece	8.36	10.64
France	7.48	9.96
Ireland	3.82	4.61
Germany	2.55	3.40
Netherlands	0.68	0.91
Belgium	0.61	0.82
Denmark	0.34	0.46
Luxembourg	0.04	0.06
Total	88.63	117.09

Source: ERDF *Twelfth Annual Report for 1986*, p. 5.

ously the theoretical maximum set at 117.09 per cent of the fund in 1986 was unattainable. Table 5.2 shows the range of national shares. The extent to which member states made use of their share beyond the minimum quota was a function of their regional problems and also of their willingness to subject their projects and programmes to control by the Commission.

After 1985 programmes became more important and it was agreed that within three years at least 20 per cent of expenditure would be devoted to integrated development programmes. These programmes are easier to assess by the Commission instead of a multiplicity of separate projects having to be examined. Programmes also lead to more coherent and co-ordinated regional development, facilitating an enhanced input by Local Authorities. There was an increased level of financing by the ERDF which was raised from 30 per cent to 50 per cent for projects and even higher (to 70 per cent) for programmes.

Programmes fell into various categories, such as Community Programmes, involving regions in more than one member state, or National Programmes of Community Interest. Post-1985 also saw the launch of Integrated Development Operational Programmes and IMPs. These

IMPs were a particular new feature which arose partly from political pressure to compensate existing Mediterranean regions for Iberian enlargement in 1986. For example, in Greece Papandreous' PASOK Party which, like the British Labour Party in the 1970s, had initially opposed the EC, imitated its tactics in demanding extra financial help to justify its continued membership of the Community.

Many innovatory aspects were manifested in the IMPs. These included an integrated approach to development, careful consideration of the environmental aspects, involvement of SMEs and the coming together of different local groups to participate in the planning process. There was to be a partnership between the region, the member state and the EC. Each contributed financially, with the major contribution being given by the Community. Some private finance was also forthcoming, mainly in France, to a lesser extent in Italy and in a minor way in Greece (G. Bianchi in Leonardi (ed.), 1993, p. 61).

The results were generally beneficial, with those regions which already possessed a planning system having no difficulty in implementing the IMPs. Most Italian regions fell into this category; for example, Umbria, Emilia-Romagna, Tuscany, Veneto, Friuli-Venezia, Guilia, March and Lazio. Those which lacked a planning system, such as Sicily, Campania and Calabria, were less successful (Leonardi (ed.), 1993, p. 235). The experience of IMPs and their deficiencies pointed the way forward in reforming the structural funds in 1988. They showed the need to concentrate spending and have a regionally balanced partnership. Without sufficient concentration of spending on the regionally integrated programmes there could only be a minimal impact.

The deficiencies were most apparent in Greece where a highly centralized political system frustrated the operation of the IMPs. At least the IMPs resulted in a re-division of the country from the 55 Prefectures down to six Regions to administer the IMPs. However, there was insufficient decentralization and still too much of a 'top down' approach by the central parties, both in planning and controlling the expenditure (with the EU money going into the national budget). Instead of properly drawn-up local plans bits and pieces were carried out, often lacking enough spending on key elements such as infrastructure; for example, in Crete, there was plenty of hotel investment, whereas what was needed was better airport facilities (F. Papageorgiou and S. Verity in Leonardi (ed.), 1993, p. 145). Although there were local people on the regional IMP Monitoring Committee, they had limited powers and felt inferior to both national and EC officials. Basically, the central administration in Athens was slow and bureaucratic, whereas those involved locally in development were operating far more actively and quickly.

Overall the IMPs constituted a step in the right direction in encouraging new regional structures. But central governments have generally been reluctant to develop appropriate administrative substructures and to relinquish their powers sufficiently, as exemplified by Greece. Also, other deficiencies in the IMPs have been highlighted in reports by the Court of Auditors, such as a lack of co-ordination between the structural funds plus the complexity of the planning procedure resulting in significant delays to spending by particular firms. In addition, there has been underuse of EIB funding.

MAJOR REFORM OF THE STRUCTURAL FUNDS, 1988

Compared with earlier reforms in 1979 and 1985, those in 1988 were the most significant of all. They followed on from the SEA in 1987 which formally incorporated regional policy into the Community. The new Regulations continued to prioritize programmes rather than projects. The 1988 reforms strengthened Community Programmes, and as a result Community Initiatives were introduced (discussed more fully at the end of this chapter). The new Regulations also developed key concepts such as concentration of expenditure, both geographically and functionally, on specific objectives. There was also to be co-ordination of the funds, partnership, additionality, and monitoring and assessment. The funds were to co-operate in a close-knit way once these changes came into effect from the beginning of 1989. The Commission's real wish was to convert the ERDF from a financing body towards a real development agency.

The main basis of the reforms was to lay down five priority Objectives for the structural funds, three of which are regional in nature (1, 2 and 5b), whilst Objectives 3, 4 and 5a are horizontal. The first Objective was the development and structural adaptation of regions whose development was lagging behind the rest. These lagging Objective 1 regions were those with GDP per head at least 25 per cent lower than the EC average. Regions are based and defined on the Nomenclature of Territorial Units for Statistics (NUTS). Different levels are used, with the main focus being on NUTS level II. Objective 1 covered the whole of Greece, Portugal and Ireland, Northern Ireland, most of southern Italy (Abruzzi, Basilicata, Calabria, Campania, Molise, Apulia, Sardinia and Sicily); also most of Spain (Andalusia, Asturias, Castile-Leon, Castile-La Mancha, Ceuta-Melilla, Valencia, Extremadura, Galicia, the Canary Islands and Murcia). French overseas territories were also included for special reasons. Altogether Objective 1 regions cover a significant geographical part territorially of the EU, but with relatively low population density applied to only 21.7 per cent of the EC's population.

Objective 1 regions tend to be characterized by insufficient development of industry and services, with above average agricultural employment. Apart from low GDP per head, they tend to have low activity rates and above average unemployment. In essence, most have failed to reach a satisfactory threshold level of development. The most fundamental elements inhibiting faster growth are the lack of adequate economic infrastructure, such as transport, and insufficient social infrastructure, such as educational qualifications and skills. There is also a general lack of entrepreneurship. As a consequence up to 80 per cent of ERDF commitment appropriations were earmarked for Objective 1 regions, with particular emphasis upon creating a proper infrastructure. Community part-financing was up to a maximum of 75 per cent of the total cost of the project and had to represent at least 50 per cent of public expenditure occasioned by the project.

The second Objective was to convert the regions or parts of regions which were seriously affected by industrial decline, and here NUTS level III applies. These regions were defined on the basis of high unemployment rates over the past three years (at least 1.25 per cent above average), and also where the share of industrial employment was above the EC average and where industrial employment had fallen. The Regulations also mentioned secondary criteria enabling the Objective 2 eligible areas to be extended to include adjacent areas which met the main criteria, to urban communities and to areas with sectoral problems. Member states had put forward some 900 areas for consideration by the Commission, which whittled these down to 60 eligible areas covering a population of over 50 million inhabitants. Emphasis was placed especially upon trying to develop productive investment both in industry and services.

The population covered under Objective 2 was about 15 per cent of the Community's population. The Regulations also provided under Objective 2 for the inclusion of Berlin. Community financing was not to exceed 50 per cent of the total cost of the project and had to represent at least 25 per cent of public expenditure occasioned by the project. The time period was set for three years.

Objective 3 was to combat long-term unemployment, covering people over 25 years old who had been out of work for more than 12 months. This Objective has subsequently been modified in the revised Regulations running from 1994–99 (details of this will be given in the next section).

Objective 4 consisted of measures to help the occupational integration of young people (less than 25 years of age). This Objective has also been altered in the revised Regulations from 1994–99, 'to facilitate workers' adaptation to industrial changes and to changes in production systems'.

Objective 5a was to speed up the adjustment of agricultural structures and Objective 5b was the development of rural areas: these comprised 17.3 per cent of EU land area and 5.1 per cent of its population. These are areas outside Objective 1 regions which have a high share of agricultural unemployment, a low level of agricultural income and a low level of socio-economic development. The Regulations also referred to secondary criteria which would permit an extension of the eligible areas on the reasoned request of the member states (depopulation, peripheral nature and sensitivity to the reform of the CAP). Community part-financing was not to exceed 50 per cent of the total cost of the project in 5b areas and had to represent at least 25 per cent of public expenditure occasioned by the project.

Whereas Objective 5a is tackled solely by the EAGGF (guidance section), Objective 5b is regional and comprises a mix of EAGGF (guidance section), ERDF and ESF expenditure. The ERDF also has the predominant role in support of Objective 1, along with the ESF and EAGGF (guidance section); and for Objective 2 the ERDF is assisted by the ESF. Objectives 3 and 4 are financed by the ESF (considered later in a separate chapter). The current contribution of each of the structural funds to the attainment of Objectives 1–5 are shown in the next section.

The location of assisted areas under Objectives 1, 2 and 5b are shown in Figure 5.1. There was a significant increase in the availability of resources with the aim of doubling in real terms the size of the structural funds between 1989 and 1993. This is shown in Table 5.3, along with the distribution between the Objectives.

The national quota system for the allocation of funding to Objective 1 regions continued with an indicative allocation in 1989, being: Greece,

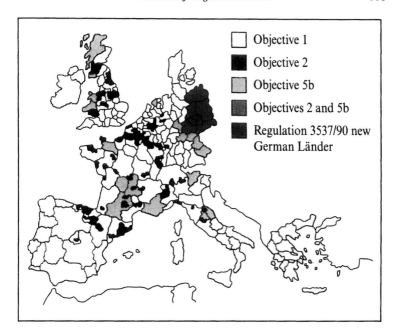

Source: CEC (1989).

Figure 5.1   EC assisted areas, 1988–93

Table 5.3   Structural funds breakdown by Objectives, 1989–93

Objective	1989–93 (in bn ECU at 1988 prices)	%
Objective 1	37.0	63
Objective 2	6.4	11
Objectives 3 & 4	7.2	12
Objective 5	6.0	10
Other	1.7	3
Total	58.3	100 (rounded up)

Source: CEC (1993d), p. 63.

16.2 per cent; Spain, 32.6 per cent; France, 2.1 per cent; Ireland, 5.4 per cent; Italy, 24.5 per cent; Portugal, 17.5 per cent; and the UK, 1.7

Table 5.4   Structural fund allocations, 1989–93 (million ECU)

	Objective 1	Objective 2	Objectives 3 and 4	Objective 5	Total
	1989–93	1989–91	1990–92	1989–93	
Belgium	–	195	174	33	402
Denmark	–	30	99	23	152
W. Germany	–	355	573	525	1,453
Greece	6,667	–	–	–	6,667
Spain	9,779	735	563	285	11,362
France	888	700	872	960	3,420
Ireland	3,672	–	–	–	3,672
Italy	7,443	265	585	385	8,678
Luxembourg	–	15	7	3	25
Netherlands	–	95	230	44	369
Portugal	6,958	–	–	–	6,958
United Kingdom	879	1,510	1,025	350	3,678
Total	36,286	3,900	4,128	2,607	46,835

Source: European Commission, Vickerman (1992).

per cent. The overall distribution between countries is shown more fully in Table 5.4.

REVISED REGULATIONS, 1994–99

Objectives 1 (and 2) remain unchanged, but the geographical coverage of Objective 1 regions has seen the inclusion of some new regions. These are shown in Figure 5.2. In Germany it includes the five new *Länder* and east Berlin; in Belgium, Hainaut; in France, the arrondissements of Valenciennes, Douai and Avesnes, given their proximity to Hainaut; in Spain, Cantabria has been added; in the Netherlands, Flevoland is now included; and in the UK, Merseyside, and the Highlands and Islands Enterprise Area. A few of these new areas qualified automatically on GDP less than 75 per cent of the EC average, such as Flevoland, with most being included for specific reasons, such as high youth unemployment. Hence Objective 1 regions now extend beyond the areas mainly in southern Europe to include declining industrial areas such as Hainaut and Merseyside which have high youth unemployment. Having redefined the areas to be covered under Objective 1

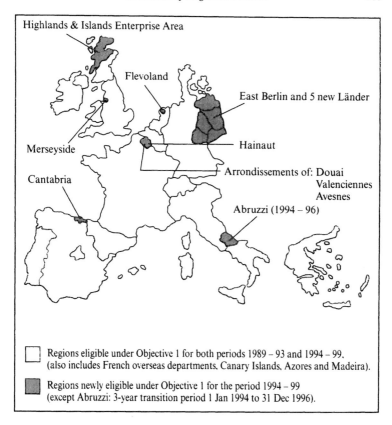

Highlands & Islands Enterprise Area

Flevoland

East Berlin and 5 new Länder

Merseyside

Hainaut

Cantabria

Arrondissements of: Douai
Valenciennes
Avesnes

Abruzzi (1994 – 96)

☐ Regions eligible under Objective 1 for both periods 1989 – 93 and 1994 – 99.
(also includes French overseas departments. Canary Islands. Azores and Madeira).

▨ Regions newly eligible under Objective 1 for the period 1994 – 99
(except Abruzzi: 3-year transition period 1 Jan 1994 to 31 Dec 1996).

Source: CEC (1993c), p. 13.

Figure 5.2   Regions eligible under Objective 1

for the next six years, no adjustments can be made to substitute other areas which have fallen on difficult times, hence rendering policy relatively inflexible.

The population covered by Objective 1 regions in the Community is 26.6 per cent (including Abruzzi for only a three year transition period until 31 December 1996). The increase over 1988 has been brought about mainly by the inclusion of the five new *Länder* in eastern Germany.

Resources available for commitment during 1994–99 (in million ECUs at 1992 prices) total ECU 141,471 million over the six years, of

Table 5.5   Commitment appropriations, 1994–99 (ECU million at 1992 prices)

	1994	1995	1996	1997	1998	1999	1994 to 1999
Structural funds and FIFG	20 135	21 480	22 740	24 026	25 690	27 400	141 471
of which: Objective 1 regions	13 220	14 300	15 330	16 396	17 820	19 280	96 346

Source: CEC (1993c).

which Objective 1 areas are to receive ECU 96,346 million. This is shown in Table 5.5.

There is to be a 74 per cent concentration from 1994 to 1999 of all the structural funds in Objective 1 areas. For the four member states also eligible for the cohesion financial instrument (Spain, Greece, Ireland and Portugal), the increase must lead to a doubling of commitment in real terms. The indicative allocation for the poorest Objective 1 areas, including Cohesion Fund allocations of ECU 15.51 billion, are that Spain will receive by far the most (ECU 36.5–38.5 billion), followed by Portugal and Greece (ECU 19.0–20.0 billion each and Ireland (ECU 8.1–9.3 billion) in the years running up to 1999. The contribution to Objective 1 regions in these four countries may rise to a maximum of 80 per cent of the total cost, and to a maximum of 85 per cent of the total cost for the outermost regions as well as for the outlying Greek islands which are severely handicapped by distance.

Table 5.6 shows the remaining allocation of funding is 6 per cent for Objective 2, 11 per cent for Objectives 3 and 4, 4 per cent for Objective 5a and 5 per cent for Objective 5b. Objective 2 is essentially unchanged, but some areas now include the impact of restructuring in the fisheries sector. Also, Objective 2 is broken down into two three-year phases with a possibility of adjusting areas and CSFs at the end of the first period: the text of the framework Regulations limits the inclusion of west Berlin to three years. For the UK, mainly affected by Objective 2 status, this applied to 19.9 million people in 1989, and under the revised Regulations to 19.1 million people (with 17.7 million people under Objective 2 and 1.4 million under Objective 1).

Table 5.6 Structural funds, 1994–96/99: financial allocations by Objective (% of total by member state)

Resources available for the CSFs		B	DK	D	GR	E	F	IRL	I	L	NL	P	UK	EUR12
Objective 1	1994–99	45	–	73	100	87	19	100	78	–	8	100	26	74
Objective 2	1994–96	10	9	4	–	4	16	–	4	9	16	–	23	6
Objective 3 and 4	1994–99	29	45	10	–	6	28	–	9	31	59	–	37	11
Objective 5a	1994–99	12	39	6	–	1	17	–	4	52	9	–	5	4
Objective 5b	1994–99	5	8	7	–	2	20	–	5	8	8	–	9	5
Total		100	100	100	100	100	100	100	100	100	100	100	100	100
Total member state as % of EUR12		1.3	0.5	14.8	11.1	24.1	9	4.5	15	0.1	1.5	11	7.2	100

Source: DG XVI.

These Objective 2 regions had to lobby strongly for continued funding since it was argued that these problems could be tackled mainly by national governments spending their own money in the richer member states. Therefore the Association of Traditional Industrial Regions (RETI) which had been formed in Lille in April 1984 brought in more industrial regions and changed its name to the Association of European Regions of Industrial Technology (retaining the acronym RETI). A meeting of 60 Objective 2 regions was held in July 1991 which in turn nominated eight regions to lobby strongly for them: these were Strathclyde (which provided the major new leadership initiative), Catalonia, Wallonia, Tuscany, North Jutland, Nord Pas-de-Calais, North Rhine-Westphalia and Groningen-Drenthe. They have lobbied not just the Commission but also national governments, the EP and the Economic and Social Committee (ECOSOC) with a successful outcome (McAleavy and Mitchell, 1994). Many regions have established offices in Brussels for lobbying purposes, either separately or alongside others. For example, Spanish regions are the latest, following the German *Länder*. Spanish regional offices in Brussels include Catalonia and the Basque country, and in addition, Galicia, Murcia, the Canary Islands and Valencia.

The most significant changes in the new Regulations have been made to Objectives 3 and 4. Objective 3 now combines the old Objectives 3 and 4. It is to combat long-term unemployment and to facilitate the integration into working life of young people and those threatened with exclusion from the labour market. The new Objective 4 gives effect to the task laid down in the Maastricht Treaty to take anticipative and preventative action to facilitate adaptation to industrial change by those already in employment.

There have been only minor changes to Objectives 5a and 5b in adding aid to modernize and restructure fisheries. Objective 5b lays down the general criteria of a low level of economic development. There are three other main criteria, of which two are necessary to satisfy conditions of eligibility: a high share of agricultural unemployment, a low level of agricultural income, a low population density and/or a significant depopulation trend. The current breakdown of the structural funds to attain Objectives 1–5b is shown below.

Objective 1   ERDF, ESF and EAGGF Guidance Section.
Objective 2   ERDF and ESF.
Objective 3   ESF.

Objective 4   ESF.
Objective 5a   EAGGF Guidance Section and FIFG.
Objective 5b   EAGGF Guidance Section, ESF and ERDF.

The revised structural funds Regulations reinforce the appraisal monitoring and evaluation procedures. They also enhance the involvement of the EP, which has to receive the lists of all the areas concerned, along with their development plans and CSFs. The EP has to be notified of Community Initiatives before they are adopted. Finally, it is provided with regular and detailed information on the implementation of the funds.

Structural funding is to rise from ECU 20,135 million in 1994 to ECU 27,400 million in 1999 (CEC, 1993c, p. 16). Also, there is the new Cohesion Fund of ECU 1.5 billion in 1993 rising to ECU 2.6 billion in 1999. The Cohesion Fund is aimed at member states (rather than regions) having GNP per head of less than 90 per cent of the EC average. It is therefore restricted to Spain, Portugal, Greece and Ireland, with indicative allocations, as with the structural funds, being: Spain, 52–58 per cent; Portugal and Greece each with 16–20 per cent; and Ireland, 7–10 per cent. Cohesion Fund spending focuses on a balance between transport infrastructure and environmental projects. The rate of funding is high at 80–85 per cent of public expenditure. The Cohesion Fund is complementary to the structural funds, but specific projects in receipt from one of the structural funds will not also be eligible for support from the Cohesion Fund.

Cohesion funding is dependent on fulfilment of the Maastricht measures to reduce public debt and budget deficits. It is partly to offset any national expenditure cutbacks brought about by these tough new budgetary conditions. Unlike the structural funds, therefore, the concept of additionality need not apply (Scott, 1995, p. 39). Also, there is no input of partnership at a lower level than that of the member states.

STRUCTURAL FUND PLANNING AT THE REGIONAL LEVEL

The member state has played the central role in co-ordinating and dispatching proposals to Brussels and then in the distribution of the finance received. Private and individual companies can apply to the ERDF, in the case of the UK via the regional offices of the Department of Trade and Industry, the Industry Department of Scotland, the Welsh Office Industrial Department, and in Northern Ireland the Department of Economic Development. Public and Local Authorities apply through the Department of the Environment. (For contact addresses see Davison and Seary (1990, pp. 47–8.)

There is a delicate balance of power between the EU, the member state and the Regional or Local Authority. In the past the member state was clearly in the driving seat and constituted the direct link between the region and the EU. Now a new relationship has started to emerge in which power is being distributed not only upwards to the EU, but also downwards to the regions. Also, the latter have started to take the initiative in dealing directly with Brussels. There is now far more interaction between the three actors, as illustrated in Figure 5.3.

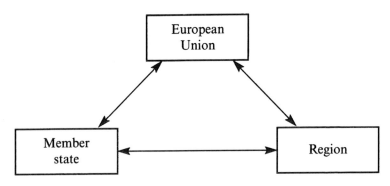

Figure 5.3   The evolving relationship between the three actors in the structural funds

The aim was to move towards a balanced triangular relationship in which the regions have enhanced powers. The new Committee of the Regions emanating from the Maastricht Agreement (and referred to in Chapter 1) exemplifies this. Also, its consultative role could be strengthened further after the IGC in 1996. Subsidiarity is important and the Regulations reinforce and extend the principle of partnership, involving close collaboration between all the relevant actors in the preparation, monitoring and evaluation of operations. The extent to which this occurs in reality depends largely on the member state being committed to greater regional involvement.

In the case of some member states, regional powers have been enhanced and devolved in recent years, whereas in the UK power has become increasingly centralized. The Conservative government has reinforced this, since its political support lies mainly in the south rather than the outlying northern regions. It has also tried to play the card of upholding a United Kingdom and is concerned about ceding further powers not only to the EU, but also to the regions. Hence the next election in the UK seems likely to be fought out not just on traditional issues, such as those of domestic economic performance, but also on federalism in the EU and devolution to the regions. The Labour Party has promised devolution, for example, a Scottish Parliament with separate fiscal powers, and the stage seems set for a real battle over Europe and the regions. This will determine whether we are to have a situation in which all regions have increased powers, including the English regions, or just in Scotland and Wales where the region is also synonymous with a separate nation. One can see either an evolving new relationship in which redistribution of power creates a new and stable equilibrium with regional contentment, or one in which a dis-United Kingdom fragments. The EU offers a perspective and opportunity in which a nation such as Scotland might choose a directly new relationship with the EU.

The stages in the structural fund process begin with the submission of a development plan for the region: this is prepared by the competent national or regional authorities. In the past most governments laid down the priorities for the development of the regions entitled to funding and drew up the development plans. One exception was Germany, where the *Länder* perform this task. One element of the new regulations is to require the planning process to take place at the regional level. This diagnoses the current situation, the finance used and the main results of past operations, along with any evaluation which is available. There is an outline with regard to its main national strategy and the Objectives which it is targeting. These are quantified where possible, with a prior appraisal of expected impact, including that on jobs, to ensure that benefits correspond to the resources used. There is also an environmental impact of the strategy and operations proposed in terms of sustainable development principles. In addition there is an indicative overall financial table summarizing the national and EU financial resources provided for, corresponding to each regional development priority, as well as an indication of the planned use of the assistance from the structural funds, the EIB and other financial instruments.

The Merseyside 2000 Plan in 1994 was just one example of several Objective 1 plans. It outlined the relative decline of Merseyside and set out eight strategic objectives. These prioritized:

- the establishment of a diverse, self-reliant, market-oriented and export-driven development of *industry and services*;
- the creation of excellent *telecommunications*;
  the improvement of:
- *R&D*, by strengthening the existing base in higher education institutions, industry and specialist bodies;
- *human resources*, by stimulating enterprise and developing skills to increase individual and regional prosperity through a human resources strategy;
- *tourism and image*, by improving the image of Merseyside and making it an attractive place for visitors;
- *environment*, by clearing up dereliction and pollution, enhancing the built environment and encouraging strong progress towards sustainable development;
- *transport*, by making Merseyside again serve as a major gateway between Europe and the rest of the world;
- *agriculture*, by conserving and enhancing rural areas.

The Plan aimed to deliver these eight objectives through 32 measures which set out objectives, scope, costs, benefits and timetable.

After consideration of the plans, the next stage is that the Commission appraises them to see whether they are consistent with the Regulations and policies laid down. Officials from the relevant DGs discuss the planned expenditure, being reluctant to see any significant diminution in their own DG's share of the total. The Commission, in close collaboration with the member state and the region, then establishes a CSF setting out funding and priorities. The CSF covers in particular the development objectives (quantified where they lend themselves to quantification), the progress to be achieved during the period concerned compared with the current situation, and the priorities adopted for Community assistance; procedures for the appraisal, monitoring and evaluation of operations to be undertaken; the forms of assistance; the indicative financing plan (with details of the amount of assistance and its source); and the duration of the assistance (Council Regulation No. 2081/93). The latter also says that the CSF may, if necessary, be revised and adjusted in the light of relevant new information and development.

The final stage used to consist of an operational programme submitted by the member state with an application for assistance, but now the procedure has been reformed in most cases to two stages. Thus member states may submit a single programming document comprising the development plan and the applications for assistance relating to it. When member states submit a single document like this, the Commission adopts a single decision incorporating the details normally set out in the CSFs and operational programmes or other forms of assistance. The aim in the revised 1994–99 Regulations has been to simplify and speed up the programming procedure. The Commission has encouraged member states to focus on broadly defined programmes, cutting the detailed analysis.

Various partners are involved in the CSF and the latter provides the operational agenda. The partners comprise central government, local government and various development agencies, training and enterprise councils (TECs), higher and further education, and the voluntary sector. Since it is not feasible for every organization to be represented, those selected have to be representative. The UK has been criticized for insufficient real partnership, especially in relation to the under-representation of trades unions. The partners set out a programme of priorities and a strategy.

The Integrated Development Operational Programmes (IDOPs) have used various criteria to score different activities according to programme objective, such as job creation, additionality and partnership. The integrated approach in one of the UK's first IDOPs in an Objective 2 area is shown in Figure 5.4. First, it identified problems and the adverse consequences which stem from these. It then set out various priority measures with results and beneficial spin-offs. The priorities are: the development of productive activities (that is, factory units, refurbishing buildings and servicing sites); the improvement of transport to help local business and tourism; and the stimulation of SMEs. An SME has less than 250 employees, an annual turnover of less than ECU 20 million and a balance sheet of less than ECU 10 million. It also has to be an independent enterprise with not more than 25 per cent owned by another company. SMEs have faced acute constraints in management, marketing, finance and new product development, and so on. Another priority is to improve the image of the area through spending on the environment, which helps to bring in new inward investment. Tourism and cultural activities are seen increasingly as beneficial since they are more labour-intensive than manufacturing industry. Finally, there is a need to improve R&D and vocational training.

An operational programme Monitoring Committee is set up and a secretariat appointed. The Monitoring Committee meets twice yearly to approve applications. In accordance with the subsidiarity principle the

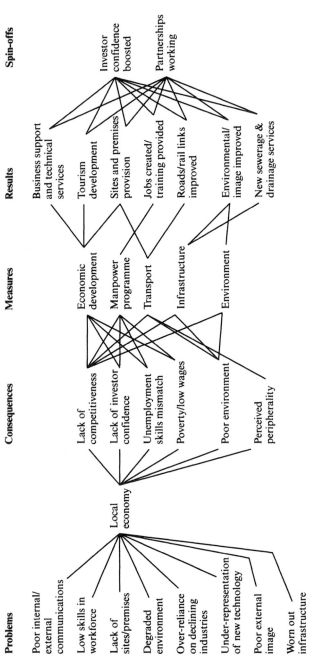

Source: Bradford District: Shaping the Future, 1994.

Figure 5.4 The integrated approach to economic regeneration

role of the Monitoring Committee has been strengthened. Without modifying the total expenditure laid down and within harmonized limits by Objective, the Monitoring Committee may adjust the procedure for granting financial assistance once this has been approved by the Commission and the member state. The secretariat informs applicants what is eligible and whether it meets the CSF priorities; for example, is it good value for money and does it pass the test of additionality? If the scheme has already started, then it will be assumed that the money is not needed and therefore is not additional. There is more chance of it being accepted as additional if it is innovative. Applicants need to prepare their applications carefully, referring to specific points in their Plan or Programme; for example, specific objectives and/or specific strategy aims, perhaps quoting page/paragraph numbers.

It is also crucial to quantify outcomes by establishing outputs, since it is these that are counted at the end. If it is claimed that a scheme will produce x number of jobs, then it is necessary that these materialize. Each phase has to have an output, but contracts can often be grouped or phased, getting each section funded. Financial claims should never be underestimated and it is necessary to allow for contingencies. Whilst you can always claim less than the amount approved, you cannot claim more. It is vital to possess copies of all relevant documentation in order to ensure you know what expenditure is eligible for ERDF assistance (and to include design fees, project administration costs, and so on). Experiences can be compared or shared with others. Response may be slow and therefore it is necessary to be patient even when further information is requested; for example, by the programme secretariat. Accurate records have to be kept of all expenditure, for at least three years, to ensure both financial control and eventually for auditing, which is conducted rigorously. Claims should be submitted regularly (for example, every quarter) instead of waiting until the project is complete. This is important since expenditure on programmes comes from Brussels in slices, and in order to draw upon subsequent slices expenditure trigger points have to be reached. The ERDF is directed almost exclusively at the public sector and the private sector in the past was not eligible to access funds since the aim was not to put money into shareholders' profits. But where the private sector has run out of money, having started but not finished a project, then it may tap into the ERDF. Also, the EU is now more favourable to private sector funding, and there have been proposals, for example, in the Merseyside 2000 Plan, for greater private sector involvement.

ERDF FINANCE: THE SPECIAL POSITION OF INFRASTRUCTURE

Finance is available for two main types of project. The first is for industrial, tourist and service activities which should create or maintain jobs. The development of indigenous potential is encouraged by measures to support local development initiatives and the activities of SMEs in particular. Help is given to construct new workshops and to create new advice centres. For tourism, other projects linked to this may be eligible, such as theatres, museums, libraries, conference centres, sports facilities and parks. For example, in Bradford in West Yorkshire the Alhambra Theatre has been refurbished and opened by Jacques Delors as part of a major phased tourism attraction. In another Local Authority in West Yorkshire a horse-drawn vehicle is used for watering hanging baskets to improve the appearance of the area for tourism which, in keeping with the application of Eurojargon, is described as mobile infrastructure.

Turning secondly to infrastructure, finance is available for roads, railways, gas, electricity, water supply and telecommunications, and so on; also R&D facilities and the building of advance factories to encourage industrial development. In Objective 1 regions, education and hospitals are also included. Particular attention has been given to transport, since the EC saw a common transport policy as being crucial to balanced development. Also, since the EC is concerned with fair competition, infrastructure investment by offering help to all participants may be seen as neutral and non-discriminatory between individual firms and industries. However, in devoting nearly 90 per cent of the ERDF expenditure to infrastructure in the past, this has tended to neglect the commitment to productive investment.

It is important to improve transport links not just between regions but also within them if poor facilities·exist and they are congested. A particular problem is that national governments and private operators favour infrastructure investment in the most developed regions where there is the greatest need and the most profits. Deregulation and privatization of transport encourages this trend further, whereas state ownership permits cross-subsidization of unprofitable routes. It is argued from the viewpoint of regional development that better infrastructure is a precondition for development in the less developed regions. However, in itself it is not the panacea (since goods can flow in more easily and labour flow out), but at least it gives them an opportunity to compete on more level terms by removing bottlenecks and improving the image of the area. In appraising infrastructure investment it is not just operator benefits but all socio-economic benefits which have to be considered in relation to costs. It is also important that expenditure is conducive to employment, but some developments, such as railway development and automatic signalling, reduce jobs.

In addition to national financing, the Community has TENs from the structural funds, also the Cohesion Fund and the EIB. It has been proposed to tap other sources of market financing; for example, by Union Bonds which would be issued (and backed by the EU budget) and convertibles (backed by the capital of the EIB). However, Britain and Germany have strongly resisted the issue of Union Bonds, since with national governmental belt-tightening these countries felt that such a borrowing campaign would set a poor example. The EU White Paper

Table 5.7 Community financing of TENs (average financing per year, 1994–99)

Source:	Amount in billion ecus	
Community budget:		**5.3**
of which:		
TENs	0.50	
Structural funds:		
(TENs):	1.35	
(environment):	0.60	
Cohesion Fund:		
(TENs):	1.15	
(environment):	1.15	
R&D:		
(telecommunications):	0.50	
(transport):	0.05	
EIB (loans):		**6.7**
Union Bonds (esp. transport and energy):		**7.0**
Convertibles guaranteed by EIF (esp. telecoms):		**1.0**
Total		**20.0**

Source: CEC (1994d), p. 33.

on Growth, Competitiveness and Employment (CEC, 1994d) proposed EU expenditure of ECU 20 billion per annum on infrastructure projects during 1994–99 to supplement private sector financing. The distribution of this expenditure on TENs is shown in Table 5.7.

The White Paper included an indicative list of 26 transport projects for consideration, ranging from a new high speed rail connection through the Brenner Pass in the Alps (estimated cost ECU 10 billion) to far more modest plans to boost inland water transport (as low as ECU 600 million). Some of the transportation projects proposed by the EU are shown in Figure 5.5.

A difficulty is in striking the right balance not only between road and rail transport, but also between strengthening connections between northern and southern Europe, and western and eastern Europe. After many years of neglecting rail transport, this has come back into fashion, largely due to the success of French TGVs. On environmental grounds there is also a strong case for promoting rail transport over further road building. However, with southern enlargement of the EC, policy has broadened to include improved shipping links and air links. Rail is most competitive with air travel for shorter journeys of up to three or four hours. Air travel has been based on linking the major cities but now with more flights from regional airports this can provide a catalyst for regional development. However, it is the development of telecommunications which will be most important in the future. This was recognized by the Special Telecommunications Action for Regions (STAR) programme in 1986, and has stimulated the supply of advanced telecommunications in the disadvantaged regions. It has included help especially for SMEs to assist them to purchase equipment to access advanced services. The peripheral underdeveloped areas have been covered by the STAR programme.

ERDF assistance occurs mainly through operational programmes, but also through part-financing of regional aid schemes, global grants, studies and technical assistance, and pilot projects. The aid is concentrated in the Objective regions, and in Objective 1 regions now includes investment in education and health, contributing to structural adjustments; and the TENs, which have received particular attention in this section. The only exception is a small amount of ERDF aid available for other purposes outside the Objective region; for example, funding some pilot activities and also a few of the Community Initiatives (which are covered in the next section).

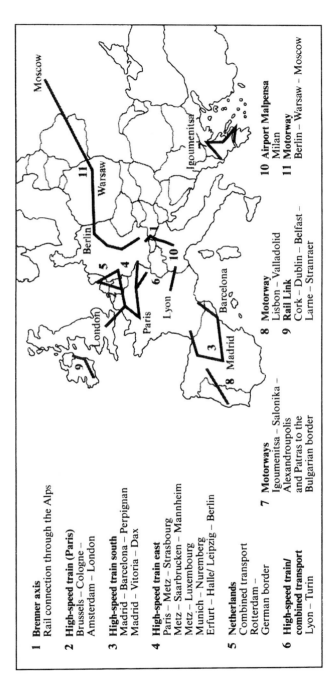

1 Brenner axis
Rail connection through the Alps

2 High-speed train (Paris)
Brussels – Cologne –
Amsterdam – London

3 High-speed train south
Madrid – Barcelona – Perpignan
Madrid – Vitoria – Dax

4 High-speed train east
Paris – Metz – Strasbourg
Metz – Saarbrucken – Mannheim
Metz – Luxembourg
Munich – Nuremberg
Erfurt – Halle/ Leipzig – Berlin

5 Netherlands
Combined transport
Rotterdam –
German border

**6 High-speed train/
combined transport**
Lyon – Turin

7 Motorways
Igoumenitsa – Salonika –
Alexandroupolis
and Patras to the
Bulgarian border

8 Motorway
Lisbon – Valladolid

9 Rail Link
Cork – Dublin – Belfast –
Larne – Stranraer

10 Airport Malpensa
Milan

11 Motorway
Berlin – Warsaw – Moscow

Source: European Union and *Wall St. Journal*, 29–30 April, 1994 p. 7.

Figure 5.5   On the road: some of the transportation projects proposed by the EU

COMMUNITY INITIATIVES

Community Initiatives have been developed, partly to offset the adverse effects of other EC policies and also to deal with other problems affecting several regions. Some 15 per cent of ERDF money was set aside for this in 1989–93, with 80 per cent earmarked for Objective 1 regions. A list of these is shown in Table 5.8 – it can be seen that the biggest Initiative in financial terms has been Interreg. This is concerned with internal border regions in the EU and also those on the external border of the EU. Those border regions outside the EU, for example in eastern Europe, have had to use Poland and Hungary Aid for Reconstruction of the Economy (PHARE). There has been concern from countries such as Greece (with no land borders with the EU) about developing maritime border links. It can be seen from the Commission Green Paper on Community Initiatives in 1993 that there was an intention to focus on five main topics for future Community Initiatives. Those proposed were:

1. Cross-border, transnational and inter-regional co-operation and networks (Interreg and Regen energy supply networks).
2. Rural development (LEADER).
3. Assistance to the outermost regions (Regis).
4. Employment promotion and development of human resources (Now, Horizon and Euroform).
5. Management of industrial change (Resider, Retex, Konver, but also Prisma, Telematique and Stride in Objective 1 regions).

The management of industrial decline has been mainly to create new jobs in alternative sectors, with expenditure by Resider in the steel industry being concentrated on job creation outside the steel industry. Apart from the decline of traditional industries, there is now also the need for diversification in regions heavily dependent on the military sector: this has been brought about by the end of the Cold War. Sectors which were formerly growth points may well experience decline comparable with that of other basic industries. However, at least the arms industry has the advantage of starting from a more advantageous position, with a strong R&D concentration and skilled manpower concentration in that sector.

The development of links between regions to tackle common problems is a useful step forward. The regions can learn from each others'

Table 5.8   Community Initiatives

Former regulations 1989–93			Revised regulations 1994–99	
List of the Community Initiatives adopted by the Commission between 1989 and 1993: (ECU million at 1989 prices)			List of the Community Initiatives adopted by the Commission between 1994 and 1999 (ECU million at 1994 prices)	
Envireg	500	Protection of the environment and development in the regions	Interreg/Regen	2,900
			Rural development	1,400
Interreg	800	Cross-border co-operation	Regis	600
Rechar	300	Diversification in coalmining regions	Employment:	
Regis	200	Integration of the most remote regions	Now	370
			Horizon	730
Stride	400	Research, technology, development and innovation in the regions	Youthstart	300
			Industrial Change:	
Regen	300	Energy networks	Adapt	1,400
Telematique	200	Advanced telecommunications services	Rechar	400
			Resider	500
			Konver	500
Prisma	100	Services to businesses in connection with the Single Market	Retex	500
			Portuguese textiles industry	400
			SMEs	1,000
Euroform	300	New skills and qualifications	Urban policy	600
Now*	120	Equal opportunities for women on the labour market	Fisheries (Pesca)	250
Horizon*	180	Access to the labour market for the handicapped and other disadvantaged groups	Reserve	1,600
			Total	13,450
Leader	400	Rural development		
Total	3,800			
Retex*		Diversification in regions dependent on the textile industry		
Konver*		Diversification in regions dependent on the military sector		

Note: *An additional sum of ECU 0.3 billion, available for Community Initiatives, was allocated to Retex and Konver – the subject of more recent decisions and for the purpose of increasing the funds earmarked for Now and Horizon.*

Source: Community Structural Funds 1994–99, CEC (1993c), p. 28. CEC (1995), pp. 5–8.

experiences. It has been argued that there is a need to develop such networking further by linking together firms in regions not necessarily joined in geographical terms, but which have common interests. For example, the Four Motors for Europe Agreement was signed in 1988 between the four regions of Rhône-Alpes, Lombardia, Catalonia and Baden-Württemburg, to which others, such as Wales, have subsequently become attached. It aims to develop transborder R&D co-operation between firms and research institutes. Networking involves flexible co-operation between firms in R&D, joint production, marketing and advertising, and so on. The EU has several programmes which are compatible with this (outlined in Table 5.8), such as Interreg, Stride, Telematique and Prisma, to which others such as Ouverture and Recite can be added. Ouverture participation involved the four regions Piedmont, Strathclyde, Sarre and Asturia, from which links with other regions have emerged in the EU and with eastern Europe. Recite was introduced in July 1991 to increase co-operation between the regions and cities of Europe. It promotes co-operation particularly in local government, including employment (within which co-operation between private sector firms also occurs). One of its main objectives is to transfer know-how and experience between the core and peripheral areas of the EU. It has been argued that since the EU has no direct urban policy both the Recite programme and the Eurocities network merit more substantial EU support (Holland, 1993). In fact, in March 1994 the Commission did adopt a proposal for a Community Initiative in the field of urban policy (URBAN).

6. Social policy problems and the role of the ESF

DEVELOPMENT OF SOCIAL POLICY

In the EU, social policy is much more narrowly defined in scope than at national level and concentrates primarily upon labour market issues. The founding of the Treaties contained a general commitment such as that of the ECSC to dealing with compensation for unemployment, retraining, health and safety, and housing. Overall, like the subsequent Spaak Committee, it was felt that there was no need for a common social policy. Thus in the Treaty of Rome there were few precise commitments, and the main emphasis was on economic integration as an end in itself. There has been considerable opportunity for national governments to block progress in the Council against the wishes of the Commission and the EP. The main pressure for a strong social policy came originally from France, which sought to prevent its own industries from becoming uncompetitive. Apart from a few cases, such as that of equal pay for women, it was considered unnecessary to introduce other measures initially since they were not distorting trade and competition.

This chapter will focus mainly on issues such as labour mobility, tackling gender inequalities in employment and the growing role of the ESF in alleviating the problem of unemployment. It will be argued that in general these policies are desirable. But there are other elements in the Social Action programmes which are questionable (apart from those such as health and safety) and run counter to employment creation.

There has been a change in emphasis over the years towards recognizing the case for a stronger social policy as an end in itself. This has arisen for a variety of reasons. It is acknowledged that there are benefits from workers participating at all levels, and with increased education this is now an expected right. In continental European countries provision has been made for workers to participate in works councils at plant level and at company board level. There are relevant provisions for co-determination in France, Denmark, the Netherlands, Luxembourg and Germany. Germany, for example, has had extensive provisions of this kind, enhancing employees' rights at the end of the Second World War since trades unions had provided a major bastion of opposition to Nazi power. Co-determination first applied in the coal and steel industry and was extended in 1976 to include joint stock companies, limited liability companies and other types of company in all sectors, provided more than 2 000 workers were employed. Since then the works director has represented the interests of the employees on the management committee. On the supervisory board, workers and salaried employees have parity representation with the shareholders. The chairman has the casting vote where the two sides are tied.

The UK was atypical of the European experience in relying mainly on confrontational, legally unregulated, collective bargaining and, in the early post-war years, on the nationalization of basic industries to improve the lot of workers. One token step towards co-determination was the setting up of the Bullock Committee (under the last Labour government) to examine the extension of industrial democracy. Although it proposed involving trades unions to a greater degree and widening representation to other interested groups, co-determination was never introduced and the change of government displaced it from the agenda. Meanwhile, in countries such as Germany the success of participation has enabled the rate of economic growth to outstrip that of the UK. Co-operation has been seen to deliver greater employee contentment and less industrial militancy. Instead of a zero sum gain where the employees' gain is the employer's loss, a variable sum situation is created which increases the total 'cake' to be shared out between the parties involved.

A preferable way forward was seen to be through the creation of appropriate institutional facilities of co-operation. This approach is reflected throughout the EU; for example, in the ECOSOC where there are representatives of workers, employers and other interested groups (but ECOSOC is only a consultative body). Co-operation between both sides of industry is also seen in the Structural Fund Committees, the ECSC Consultative Committee and the Standing Committee on Employment, which meets two or three times a year and has been concerned in the past with reducing unemployment through re-organization of working time and through vocational training. Regular Tripartite Conferences have taken place each year between trades unions, employers and the Commission. An important stimulus to co-operation between both sides of industry came from the meeting at Val Duchesse in Brussels in 1985, which initially set up two working groups, one dealing with macroeconomic problems and the other with training and new technologies.

Concern for the position of workers in society clearly reflects the strength of the political party in power nationally, along with the influence which is exercised through EU bodies such as the Council and the EP. Also, the position of the Commission in initiating new policies has been significant, particularly under the last long-serving President, Jacques Delors, a powerful Socialist politician appointed to his position by Mitterrand in France. In the UK the hostility towards the trades unions has come mainly from the Conservative Party, in continuous office since 1979. The Thatcher government learnt from the defeat inflicted on the Heath government in its attempt to reform industrial relations. Instead of proceeding to anti-union legislation all at once, during the 1980s a whole series of measures was introduced gradually, some of which were unobjectionable in themselves, such as secret ballots, but taken together represented a significant shift in the balance of power against organized labour in the UK. During the years of opposition the British Labour Party has modified its own position in relation to key issues such as union power, privatization and membership of the EU. The Labour Party feels more at home with the views of Socialist governments and with an EU which it perceives to have become increasingly focused on a Social Europe. This change in attitude is reflected by Neil and Glenys Kinnock who opposed the concept of Europe as a capitalist market, but now fully endorse a new Social Europe and are active participants in its creation.

The pressure to enhance European social policy has become necessary to complement the balance with the earlier and almost over-riding emphasis on establishing a market in which only business benefited. The whole Single Market programme activated by Delors in the late 1980s, to be achieved by 1992, sparked off the degree of interaction which was to exist between the social and market elements. For example, in the UK Mrs Thatcher was delighted by the prospects of developing a Single Market, which she believed reflected the triumph of her liberal principles, but was aghast when this was linked with extensive measures for social policy.

Concern to develop a stronger social policy has also arisen to create some counterbalance to multinational companies which have grown in importance and in the ability to exploit workers who are not protected by social legislation. The phrase 'social dumping' came into fashion as those countries with higher social costs and greater social protection became worried about the loss of jobs. Trades unions, in particular in northern Europe, saw jobs being likely to move in large numbers to southern Europe where the costs and degree of social protection are much weaker. The Commission recognized that the main problem was confined to labour-intensive sectors which were relatively unskilled, such as foodstuffs, road and maritime transport, and the building trade. To limit any social unfairness the Commission proposed that, in order to help the local workforce, where a public building contract was awarded to a contractor from another member state, the contractor must apply the social welfare conditions and wage agreements established in the country where the work is to be carried out. There will be even greater concern in the context of social dumping in relation to exploiting low cost labour in eastern Europe. However, many economists consider that social dumping would actually be beneficial for economic development and only market forces will be able to develop weaker areas.

In achieving a more extensive social policy in the EU, progress is restrained by a variety of obstacles. Clearly those who believe in the operation of markets object in principle to intervention, particularly when applied in a uniform way across disparate economies. Furthermore, at a time when macroeconomic policy is also becoming integrated increasingly at an EU level, and therefore restricting flexible national instruments, one might argue that labour markets should remain largely competitive and not be unduly regulated. The UK government in particular has difficulties not only with EU social policy but also with EMU, regarding both as too restrictive on the management of its own affairs.

There are objections to moving to qualified majority voting on more social policy issues. There is also worry about these turning into Regulations, whereas the reality is that most are enabling measures, opening the way to future Directives (which are more flexible); also, other elements consist of Regulations and Opinions (Wise and Gibb, 1993, p. 188). The main exceptions relate to gender equality and health and safety, where the UK was in agreement that majority voting would apply to these matters. It has led to some EU plans, such as those to limit the working week, being promoted under Article 118a on health and safety, whereas the UK has fundamental objections to them, the UK having no restrictions itself on working hours. Whereas overtime working is restricted to an extra two hours maximum per day in some EU countries, no such legislation has existed in the UK and overtime working is widespread.

Apart from opposition by the Conservative government in the UK on ideological grounds to social policy being introduced through the European back door, employers in some other EU countries also have reservations over particular measures and are in a stronger position than trades unions. For example, employers are represented in UNICE (the Industrial Confederation of the EC, which was formed at the inception of the EC), whereas the European Trade Union Confederation (ETUC) was only formed in 1973 and excluded Communist unions. Employers are having to compete in an international market-place and if they are weighed down by increased social costs which are not borne by non-EU employers, then unemployment will continue to rise. In fact, the main constraint on EC social policy-making, with its ambitions to create full and enriching employment, has been brought about by recessions since the early 1970s.

LABOUR MIGRATION

One of the fundamental freedoms of the EU is that of free movement of labour, and it has been necessary to ensure that individuals and families who move are not treated unfairly and in a discriminatory fashion. This section will examine the scale of migration, the reasons underlying it, its overall effects and prospective trends. The statistics on migration need to be handled carefully. Those relating to gross migration show that this is very substantial, with large numbers of people moving between and into EU countries. However, not all migrants stay, even though *ex post* the tendency to stay far exceeds *ex ante* intentions. Native-born citizens also emigrate to other countries. It is therefore usual to use statistics of net migratory flows, which are much smaller. A main measure used is the number of foreign residents as a percentage of the population. These official figures naturally exclude those immigrants who have become naturalized citizens; also excluded are illegal immigrants. Statistics of foreign residents as a percentage of the population reveal that not only do these tend to be relatively low in EU member states, but within nine of the 12 countries the percentage of non-EU immigrants is a higher percentage of the resident population than that of intra-immigrants. These are shown in Table 6.1.

Table 6.1   Distribution of EC residents by country of origin (%)

	Non-EC	Other EC	National
Belgium	3.3	5.4	91.3
Denmark	2.1	0.5	97.3
France	3.8	2.8	93.4
Germany, West	5.2	2.1	92.7
Greece	1.1	1.1	97.8
Ireland	0.5	1.9	97.3
Italy	0.6	0.2	99.3
Luxembourg	1.9	23.9	74.2
Netherlands	3.0	1.1	96.0
Portugal	0.7	0.2	99.1
Spain	0.4	0.5	99.1
UK	1.8	1.3	96.9
EC	2.5	1.5	96.1

Source: *Eurostat*, Luxembourg: OOPEC, 1991.

Emigration has been more significant as a percentage of population for countries such as Ireland, with the Thomson Report (CEC, 1973) showing that, before joining the EU, from 1961–71 Irish emigration was 141,600. Emigration from Italy 1960–69 was 517,900. Southern enlargement of the EU in the 1980s brought in other countries such as Portugal which has been a major country of emigration. Within the EU the expectation was that the pattern of migration would increase within the EU because of free movement and the tendency of migrants to switch the country of destination from outside to inside the EU. In practice, however, most migration has tended to come from extra-EU sources rather than intra-EU sources. A major explanation of this is that integration through the movement of goods and labour has tended to equalize factor earnings within the EU. By contributing to a higher plateau of economic growth in the EU compared with countries out-side, it has provided a magnetic attraction to immigrants from outside.

Workers traditionally have emigrated partly because of 'push' factors domestically, such as overpopulation, leading to unemployment and poverty. In addition to economic difficulties there have often been political pressures of persecution. These are not sufficient causal fac-tors in themselves, since for migration actually to take place they have to be accompanied by 'pull' factors in the countries of destination. Emigration has always tended to run in parallel to high demand for labour in the economies to which migrants wish to move. Migrants evaluate all the expected relative benefits from moving compared with staying put, minus the costs involved. The latter comprise both financial costs and the non-pecuniary aspects, such as learning a new language and culture. Clearly, costs and benefits vary at different times of life. The benefits are greatest if one moves when young and single since one can maximize earnings over a longer time span, and it is easier to integrate. Some countries have experienced more temporary immigration of single workers (the *gastarbeiter*, as in Germany). This practice of the influx of guest workers being used as the marginal element to be removed in recession has become complicated in recent years when such workers have been followed by their wives and children. In fact, the benefits of migration are best considered from the perspective of the household, since migrant husbands tend to benefit far more from higher earnings than their wives. In the UK and France immigration has conformed more closely to a pattern of family settlement. Many have come from former Empire territories, resulting in them being considered worthy of citizenship.

Migration has been a function of the overall demand for labour and also the supply response of indigenous workers whose preferences have moved away from relatively unrewarding dirty manual jobs. The effects of migration can be examined from the viewpoint of both the host country and the countries of origin. The economic effects on the host country depend upon whether immigrants add more to supply or to demand. Immigration shifts the supply curve of labour to the right, lowering the general level of wages, initially adversely affecting indigenous workers who have tended to be hostile to immigration, even more so during periods of recession. In Figure 6.1 the effects are shown diagramatically to illustrate the division of national income between labour and capital. Total income is shown under the demand curve, D_1, in which capital receives the triangular area ABD, whilst labour receives the remainder of income, $OABL$. Immigration of labour, LM, shown by a new labour supply curve, S_2, lowers wages to OC, with labour's share of income shown by the rectangle $OCEM$. Capital receives the enlarged triangular income, CDE. Immigrants are usually concentrated in the secondary industrial sector where productivity is high and, being prepared to work flexible and long hours, they are conducive to ensuring high profits. They act like Marx's general re-

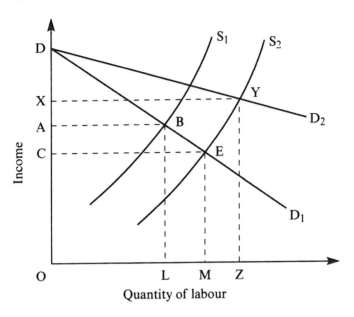

Figure 6.1   The economic effects of immigration on host countries

serve army of labour. The static situation, then, is one in which wages fall.

However, dynamically immigration has far-reaching effects since it is likely to shift demand for labour to the right. This is because with higher profits the capital stock is increased as a result of higher indigenous investment plus inward multinational investment to the host country. The marginal product of labour increases and a new demand curve is shown as D_2. The effect has been to enlarge total national income, shown as *ODYZ*, employing even more labour, *MZ*. It can be seen in Figure 6.1 that capital enjoys the enlarged triangular income of *XDY*. In the new situation wages may also rise, in this case from *OC* to *OX*, and labour's share of national income has risen to *OXYZ*. In this scenario, therefore, continued economic expansion is feasible since both capital and labour may benefit, with continued pressure to absorb increased immigrant labour.

A less favourable outcome would be where the existing capital stock was not increased but was shared out between more employees, with a decline in the capital ratio and in output per head (productivity). Instead of any capital deepening taking place, the little investment which occurs tends to be mainly capital widening. Firms use the same production techniques, and smaller and less efficient firms may be kept in business using cheap labour. One example of this has been in the textile industry, in which immigration has helped to hold down labour costs and maintain temporary competitiveness, but in the long run can never compete on labour costs with imports from NICs with their even lower labour costs. Immigrants also make demands on social capital, such as housing and education. In relation to social security they have tended to draw out less than the indigenous population, partly as a function of their lower age and lower pension payments. Overall, then, from an economic perspective, immigration is beneficial where supply exceeds demand, dampening inflation and improving the balance-of-payments position. However, immigration is worthy of consideration beyond economic factors because of its social and cultural implications, necessitating appropriate policies on assimilation, integration or separate development.

The effects of emigration on those who leave may be considered generally beneficial for individuals who have achieved their intentions and bettered themselves, even though the streets may not have been paved with gold as they expected. The effects on the country of origin have been to reduce the problems of overpopulation, excess labour supply and unemployment. Reducing oversupply of labour has tended to improve wages for those left behind. Much hinges upon the type of labour which leaves, and clearly the more it consists of skilled labour, the greater is the drain of human capital which has been tied up in education and training by poorer countries. In the short term, migrants send home remittances to their families which provide a source of investment and also help to reduce the balance-of-payments deficit. In the long run, the return of the migrants themselves is more beneficial as they return with enhanced skills and familiarity with newer industrial methods. Overall, though, it would appear that the economic benefits for the countries receiving labour are far in excess of those in the countries of origin, where the exodus from the latter has been on such a scale as to decimate particular communities.

Prospective trends in migration are a function of demographic factors which continue to be favourable. There is strong population pressure in many less developed countries, such as north Africa with a 2.5 per cent per annum population growth. Meanwhile, in the EU the birth rate has fallen and the number of young people under 25 years of age in the workforce is likely to decline in the order of some 25 per cent by the end of the century. This could create demand for up to another 10 million immigrants. In addition, the end of the Iron Curtain separating eastern Europe and the introduction of economic reforms there have created some additional intolerable pressures, with open unemployment emerging on a large scale. If economic reforms in eastern Europe do not succeed, then the pressure to emigrate to the west will become even more attractive. However, such economic migration will not be acceptable against a continuing background of high domestic unemployment in EU member states. Also, most of the grounds for seeking political asylum from eastern Europe have now been removed with the introduction of democracy and elevation of human rights. Demand for labour in many sectors in the EU labour market has fallen, with industries becoming more capital-intensive rather than labour-intensive. Also, the kind of labour required is increasingly skilled, better educated and needed on a permanent and not on a rotating basis. These characteristics apply especially to the rapidly growing service sector in the EU.

The EU is in a dilemma since its concern with intra-migration has been overwhelmed by extra-migratory pressures. Once immigrants have gained entry into the Union, movement is easy, and there are worries about the inability of countries such as Italy to control external borders properly. The Schengen Agreement in 1985 (France, Germany and Benelux) agreed on facilitating movement, but ran into problems over movement of people from outside, even those from eastern Germany. If the EU is to restrict immigration tightly from outside, then it has to offer some alternative to non-members to persuade them to stay at home. This can consist of freer trade for their exports, though some member states are reluctant to remove many trade restrictions. There is also an argument not just for increased trade but to accompany this with an enhanced aid package. Instead of importing unwanted labour in the future, EU member states need to combine greater overseas aid with increased private capital investment overseas. This would constitute part of a longer-term development strategy.

EU policy has evolved through various phases: it started from the concern of employers who were short of labour, then turned to focus on the rights of workers who wished to move. EU workers no longer needed work permits and were given the right to move in search of work, to settle, to bring their families, for their children to receive schooling, and to receive basic social rights. Most of the workers who moved were unskilled or semi-skilled. There is now a reduced demand for this type of migrant labour, with economic change creating a greater demand for skilled and professional workers, hence the need to harmonize qualifications and their mutual recognition. Whilst there has been considerable progress in achieving this in various professions, such as the Health Service, obstacles remain. Another change has involved the rights not just of workers, but those who are non-active, such as students, whose movement has been encouraged by the Erasmus Programme, and pensioners often moving to benefit from a warmer climate, such as British pensioners in Spain.

The EU has begun to replace the word 'migrant' by that of 'citizen', with various citizenship rights being enshrined and laid out in the Maastricht Treaty. With such developments, clear demarcation is being drawn between EU citizens and those outside. Yet the main potential for destabilizing migratory flows is likely to come from outside the EU. The economic gap between the EU and other developing economies provides a natural attraction, whilst in many countries political persecution has led people to emigrate to seek political asylum. The EU has recently taken steps on asylum, with countries in which asylum seekers first arrive being given primary responsibility.

GENDER INEQUALITIES

There has been a dramatic increase in the number of women participating in labour market employment. However, it can be shown that there are still considerable inequalities between men and women in employment, unemployment and incomes. Despite Community Initiatives and measures focused mainly on improving the position of women in the labour market, women are still disadvantaged at work and more especially in society as a whole.

The increased participation of women, particularly married women, in labour market work was stimulated initially by labour shortages during the World Wars. It showed that women were capable of doing jobs which had traditionally been thought of as men's work. Society, through its ideology, required women to fulfil roles which were expected of them. Unlike the situation between the Wars, with mass unemployment, post-1945 saw a continuing high demand for labour. This was accompanied by changes in the pattern of employment, with a larger public sector and increased white collar work. The change in attitudes to paid labour market work by married women and by their husbands has created a permanent transformation of family participation in the labour market.

The growth of female employment has been facilitated by a marked change in family size. The number of children per family has fallen sharply, with parents concentrating instead on an improved quality of provision. Children are increasingly expensive to bring up and parents no longer see them as an investment as in more traditional societies. Mothers have more time, with fewer children and an array of labour-saving devices in the home, to enable them to engage in paid labour market work.

The preference to switch from unpaid household work to paid labour market work was clearly encouraged further by increased rates of pay and measures of legislative equality. Economic analysis has shown that for women there has been a strong positive work substitution effect, which has outweighed the negative income effect to seek leisure because of higher husbands' earnings. Women's labour force participation has also changed, moving closer to that of men in terms of age participation. In the past there was a marked difference, with female participation often having a single peak for women in their early twenties, from which it afterwards declined. This partly gave way to twin peaks (a kind of M-shape) in which women, having brought up their families, returned to work. This M-pattern still fits countries such as the UK and Germany, though it is a less pronounced pattern in the 1990s than in the 1960s. Generally, the life cycle pattern of female labour supply has begun to conform towards the inverted U-shape manifested by males, with participation no longer falling but rising with age until retirement. Denmark, for example, with the highest female participation rate, is a good example of this pattern.

The female participation rates in the EU vary from 78.3 per cent in Denmark down to the lowest rate of 37.6 per cent in Ireland. Participation rates tend to be higher in northern European countries than in southern European countries (see Table 6.2).

The gap between male and female participation rates is closing not only because of the rise in female participation, but also because of the fall in male participation rates. Economists have applied the phenomenon of the backward-bending supply curve to males who have shown a negative gross wage elasticity. In contrast, studies show that the female labour supply is still positively sloped.

The pattern of employment, however, reveals a major distinction between males and females in terms of the hours worked, with a much greater degree of part-time working carried out by women. The highest percentage is in the Netherlands, where 57.7 per cent of women are

Table 6.2   Gender and the labour force

	Men	Women
Belgium	72.5	51.4
Denmark	90.3	78.3
France	75.4	55.7
Germany	82.9	54.4
Greece	75.6	43.4
Ireland	83.9	37.6
Italy	77.8	44.0
Luxembourg	88.2	47.6
Netherlands	81.1	52.0
Portugal	85.1	59.7
Spain	77.4	39.9
UK	86.8	65.2

Note:
1988: Belgium, Denmark, France, Germany, Greece, Luxembourg.
1989: Italy, the Netherlands, Portugal, Spain, UK.

Source: S. Holland (1993, Table 3.8).

part-time, though part-time work by men is also much higher in the Netherlands than elsewhere, with 14.5 per cent working part-time. The EU average showed 28.1 per cent of women engaged in part-time work, compared with 3.9 per cent of men working part-time (*Eurostat*, OOPEC, 1991). The high level of part-time work by women has been attributed to their personal preference in fitting in well with bringing up a family. However, closer inspection reveals it is not only those in midlife but also many women over 50 who work part-time. So it cannot be explained solely in terms of children, since most of these have grown up by time the mother passes the age of 50. The high degree of part-time working by women means that they are not fully utilizing their investment in skills. It represents a passive response to demand by employers for flexibility in modern production and service activities, with women being preferred mainly because they are cheaper to employ and are offered less employment protection as part-timers.

Turning to unemployment amongst women, this is significantly higher than that of male unemployment in all EU countries, apart from the UK, as shown in Figure 6.2. Unemployment amongst women is naturally

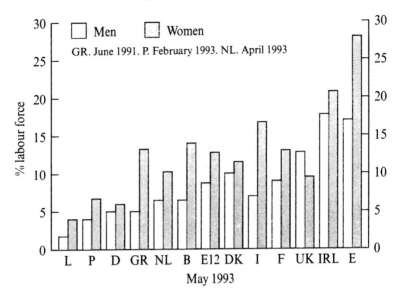

Source: CEC (1994f), p. 42.

*Figure 6.2   Unemployment of men and women in EU member states,
1993*

more difficult to calculate precisely than that of males when women leave employment and return to household work. Nevertheless, unemployment amongst women tends to be raised by a number of elements. With lower training and less investment in skills, they have greater likelihood of being laid off, especially where a 'last in, first out' principle applies. Married women experience greater frictional unemployment as a consequence of movements in and out of the labour market to produce children. Married women also have less occupational and geographical mobility (being tied to husband's location), resulting in greater structural employment. Women employed in manufacturing industry are particularly prone to unemployment cyclically. Furthermore, there is a tendency for unemployment of a married woman to accompany that of her husband's unemployment. A discouraged worker effect prevails, with the benefit system often unfortunately reinforcing family unemployment.

The most favourable feature is the greater stability of employment in the tertiary sector in which women are well represented. But employment is highly segregated, with women's jobs clustered horizontally into a relatively small number of low paid sectors. These tend to be in the secondary labour market and are often characterized by repetitive and relatively low skilled work, with a lack of promotion opportunities. Even within many of the sectors in which women predominate, such as health, education and office work, women tend vertically to be concentrated at the bottom in the lower grades and less well paid positions. To tackle this, the ESF has pursued an innovatory approach in helping to train women to fill jobs in which they have been traditionally underrepresented, and in particular to encourage increased female working in southern Europe.

Discrimination has been rampant, not only in the labour market but throughout society. Women, despite equal pay legislation and minimum wage legislation in many countries, still receive lower pay than men. Part of this can be attributed to supply-side differences such as education and training, but even after standardizing for this, a significant difference in wages remains which can only be attributed to outright discrimination by employers. It can be seen, therefore, that progress towards imposing equal pay is insufficient in itself without also tackling the issue of improved education and training for women. Once this has improved, then equal pay can operate more successfully, though it may be that some employers, who do not believe that marginal productivity between males and females has been equalized fully, will choose at the margin to employ fewer females.

A first step by the EU to provide training for women was adopted after 1971, with the ESF concentrating on training women over 35 years of age. After 1975 in particular new pilot schemes were adopted in order to prepare mature women to return to work. Furthermore, following the Council Decision in December 1977, the ESF helped to finance vocational training schemes for women over 25, with those under 25 being covered by the schemes for young people. The continued priority in improving training for women is important since many industrialized countries have tended in the past to train women for jobs which were soon to become obsolete, whereas men were trained for the new technology. By 1989 about two-fifths of all beneficiaries were women, compared with about a third of female beneficiaries between 1978 and 1983.

There have been many EU Directives covering equal pay, equal opportunities in employment, recruitment, promotion and training, and in equal treatment in social security. Its various action programmes have increasingly recognized the links between employment, maternity leave and childcare. A Directive in 1990 laid down 14 weeks' maternity leave, though with the recognition that intervention is primarily that of national governments. The maximum duration of maternity leave in 1990 was above 14 weeks in all countries, apart from Portugal at 13 weeks. It was most generous in Denmark at 28 weeks, and along with provision for parental leave further underpins the high female work participation there. Equally important is not just the length of maternity leave, but also the financial compensation offered. In some countries maternity compensation fully replaces the gross wage, for example, in Belgium, Luxembourg, the Netherlands, Portugal and Germany, the lowest compensation (60 per cent) being in Ireland. The passing of the European Pregnancy Directive in 1992 protects women, both full- and part-time, who cannot be dismissed or treated in other detrimental ways on the grounds of pregnancy. Should this occur, then they are able to claim unfair dismissal and compensation.

In addition to a major constraint created by insufficient childcare facilities, there are increasing demands on women as a result of expenditure cutbacks in care for elderly relatives. Given the continued inequality in the sharing of household chores, it means that being married still creates unequal opportunities for women. Those unable to go out to work sometimes engage in homeworking, which is notoriously badly paid with no protective rights.

Decisions by the European Court of Justice have had major implications in establishing rights to equality. Article 119 was interpreted by the European Court of Justice in 1971 in the case of *Defrenne* vs *the Belgian State*, when a stewardess employed by Sabena (the Belgian state airline) challenged her differential pay and less favourable pension arrangements. The definition of pay has gradually been extended by the European Court of Justice in its judgements to include all items of pay, such as redundancy and pensions. In 1986 the Marshall case from the UK led to the ruling that women who work in the public sector could not be forced to retire at an earlier age than men. Furthermore, in September 1994 the Court ruled that part-time employees were eligible to participate in pension schemes. However, it also ruled that those employers who paid a reduced pension to women who retire at 60 are not acting illegally. Complete equality, whilst beneficial for women, does have a downside. For example, with a common retirement age it means women having to work longer than at present and contributing more towards their pensions than in the past.

ESF: ITS CHANGING EMPHASIS

The ESF was established by the Treaty of Rome in 1957 with the aim of 'rendering the employment of workers easier and of increasing their geographical and occupational mobility within the Community'. The first ESF (1958–71) therefore placed great emphasis upon labour mobility since there was a high demand for labour in most countries, particularly Germany, with the main reservoir of unemployment being in southern Italy. Between 1961 and 1972, ESF financing enabled the re-employment of more than 1.1 million jobless, including 850,000 Italians. The ESF paid travelling expenses to the place of work and also financed cultural and language-learning classes for migrant workers and their families. These classes have taken place in the host countries and also in the country of origin prior to the migrants' leaving. Mastery of the language is crucial, facilitating access to training and providing opportunities to move beyond basic unskilled work. The ESF trained, for example, 100,000 Italians in Apulia alone for jobs in Germany, France and Belgium, and it was these countries conducting the training which were the main beneficiaries from the ESF. There was a belief at that time in the labour market largely being self-adjusting. Also, member states were mainly in control with the Commission lacking power, so that all the schemes which met the conditions had to be accepted; this resulted in resources being spread too thinly.

The second ESF (1971–83) decided on its own spending (not just that committed by member states) and would finance not only public bodies but also private ones. It was given a bigger budget and 90 per cent of this was devoted to vocational training and advanced training; it also gave a temporary wage top-up in economically backward regions. It focused on problem industries such as agriculture and textiles, whilst the ECSC continued to cover coal and steel. All the familiar categories were covered, such as migrants, women and the young unemployed (under 25 years of age), with particular emphasis on training programmes to facilitate the transition from school into employment.

The third ESF (1983–88) provided more regional concentration of assistance. Initially 40 per cent of the funds went to priority regions, and from the beginning of 1986 this increased to 44.5 per cent after enlargement of the Community. The other 55.5 per cent of the funds went to areas of high and long-term unemployment and/or areas undergoing industrial or sectoral re-organization. Most of the aid went to young people under 25, since in 1984 one in four young people were out of work. The funds focused on young people were not to drop below 75 per cent of all the available funds in any particular year (whereas in 1982 the figure for young people was only 40 per cent). A maximum of 5 per cent of funds was allocated to innovatory schemes or to investigate the efficiency of fund schemes. There was priority on vocational training for the under-18s, with courses lasting at least 800 hours (including at least 200 hours but no more than 400 hours work experience) and offering worthwhile employment prospects in priority regions. The UK during 1984–89 received ECU 2.9 billion to help 3.5 million young people, whilst Italy received ECU 2.6 billion to help 2.5 million young people and Spain received ECU 1.4 billion for 1.6 million young people. In the UK, for example, the most important scheme was the Youth Training Scheme (YTS). Figures of youth unemployment were at a peak in 1984 and have been declining since, though the figure is still high and well above unemployment in the working population as a whole. For instance, youth unemployment in 1989 was over 30 per cent in Italy, Spain and Greece, 20 per cent in Belgium and France, but only 5.5 per cent in Germany. The under-25s comprise nearly half of the unemployed in Italy, Spain and Portugal.

Reforms in the fourth ESF (1989–93) went beyond the ESF itself. These integrated the ESF into EC structural policies to increase cohesion, particularly in lagging regions. Apart from boosting regional development it focused on a smaller number of aims, but with its main principles being concentration, programming, partnership and additionality. It was particularly important to ensure the complementarity of ESF assistance with other sources of funding. In addition, the ESF became involved in several Community Initiatives (referred to in Chapter 5 and Table 5.8). These included Euroform, Now and Horizon.

The fifth ESF (1994–99) included further reforms, mainly because ESF expenditure has made only a limited impact on unemployment outside Objective 1 regions. Whilst the other structural funds were essentially operating satisfactorily, requiring more continuity than change, the ESF has seen fundamental reform, particularly in relation to redefining Objectives 3 and 4. Objective 3 is now a bigger category, including young and old. It concentrates on the occupational re-integration of the long-term unemployed back into jobs through the following measures: vocational training, pre-training (including upgrading of basic skills), and guidance and counselling; temporary employment aids; and the development of appropriate training and employment and support structures, including the training of necessary staff and the provision of care services for dependants. The occupational employment of young people is also facilitated through all the measures just mentioned. In addition, young people are to receive up to two years of vocational training leading to qualifications. The new Objective 3 now comprises all the groups socially excluded. These include the handicapped, immigrants/refugees, single parent families, the homeless, prisoners and ex-prisoners, and young people (including drug addicts). The main change is that support is to be given not just to those who are already long-term unemployed, but to those who are vulnerable to this and who are suffering from social exclusion. It is necessary, for example, to prevent these groups from drifting into unemployment. There is more flexibility for those not unemployed for a full 12 months, but who are confronted by the prospect of long-term unemployment. Specific reference is made to equal opportunities for men and women (including childcare facilities). Focus is placed particularly on areas of work in which women are under-represented and especially on women not possessing vocational qualifications or not returning to the labour market after a period of absence. For details of the amendments to the ESF see Council Regulation No. 2084/93.

A new Objective 4 has been created which helps those already in employment, but taking anticipative and preventative action to facilitate workers' adaptation to industrial change. It is general and a horizontal measure, not benefiting single firms or particular industries. It targets those already in work, giving special attention to SMEs. It offers help through the anticipation of market trends and vocational qualifications; vocational training and retraining, guidance and counselling; and assistance for the improvement and development of appropriate training systems.

The ESF pursues active supply-side policies of training and retraining, and in Objective 1, 2 and 5b regions offers additional features. It supports employment growth and stability through guidance, counselling and training, including support for training systems such as training of instructors and the improvement of employment services. It also tries to boost human potential in research and science and technology, especially through post-graduate training and the training of managers and technicians at research establishments. Objective 1 regions still constitute the main focus of attention, with a new dimension being to strengthen the education and training assistance there; for example, by training teachers in secondary schools. This needs to be linked to vocational training and training in new technology, and so on. Links between training centres or higher educational establishments is also encouraged where there is a clear link with the labour market, new technology or economic development. In Objective 1 regions training of public officials is supported where this is necessary for the implementation of development and structural adjustment policies. Maastricht Articles 126 and 127 are very relevant and reflected in the ESF. Having a partner in other regions is helpful, with increased co-operation between training establishments. Expenditure by the ESF is mainly for training but also for education systems, such as in Objective 1 regions, and since they are intertwined it is increasingly difficult to separate them.

Fund assistance may be granted towards eligible expenditure to cover: the remuneration and related costs and the subsistence and travel costs of persons covered by the operations; the preparation, operation, management and evaluation costs of activities, after deduction of revenue; and the cost of employment aid granted under arrangements existing in the member states. Capital expenditure which the ESF finances is negligible apart from, for example, altering buildings for the disabled or replacing depreciating equipment used for ESF training. It is important for claimants not just to have clear objectives which enable finance to be obtained: this then has to managed and spent properly. To this end the ESF, whilst allowing more subsidiarity, has developed increased monitoring, control and evaluation. Evaluation is both a form of stocktaking and, more positively, a tool for improving the operation of the programme. Some evaluation exercises conducted by the ESF have shown that training *per se* is insufficient; for example, it was recommended that more attention should be given to greater guidance and counselling and increased emphasis on measures directly to recruit workers into employment.

There are beneficial externalities from training the workforce and it is important that workers in the EU are equipped with the necessary skills to enable them to compete effectively in the global industrial markets. Left to private industry, companies are reluctant to train workers in general skills, preferring instead to poach labour from elsewhere. There are significant gains from filling the skills gap in which employers are getting a lower level of efficiency and providing a poorer service to customers. Employers benefit from increased productivity from higher technical ability, resulting in a multi-skilled workforce flexibly deployed plus less downtime for repair of machinery. Employees also benefit from productivity gains with increased income, better morale and shorter spells of unemployment. It is larger employers which tend to train most in particular sectors, with little training in industries such as textiles and clothing. The best time to provide this increased investment in human capital is during recession, reducing the excess supply of labour and ensuring that labour is better educated and trained ready for economic recovery. The ESF has therefore played an important role in financing training and retraining at all levels; for example, training for the unemployed, training for school leavers aimed towards recognized qualifications, and so on. ESF resources are having to be used in higher education, for instance, to retrain graduates with skills in other fields where vacancies exist, such as electronics. Under the new Objective 4, training is for those already in employment but whose jobs are threatened by industrial change.

The ESF has often operated in a slow and cumbersome manner and sometimes its funds have been stretched, with payment only made at the end of the time period and with uncertainty about continued funding. Unfortunately, as in the case of the ERDF, much of the funding (apart from innovatory expenditure) has been treated not as additional money, but has gone into financing existing government training schemes. Nevertheless, the ESF has taken a progressive view in recognizing the value of training to acquire new technical skills. In contrast, some member states have preferred to follow a short-term perspective, succumbing to pressure to support jobs in declining sectors, yet these generally offer no long-term future. The Regulations underpinning the structural funds provide more coherence and concentration of funding, providing guaranteed finance under the multi-annual programming. However, with its operations now based on partnership between those involved, this may mean that the ESF will be less able to impose its preferences in specific instances, and instead it is pre-occupied more with monitoring, controlling and evaluating the expenditure undertaken.

THE EVOLUTION OF SOCIAL POLICY UP TO MAASTRICHT

Social policy has not received the same impetus to development as that in other areas, for example, agriculture. This is partly because social policy is much more diffuse, covering a patchwork of issues from migration to gender equality and employment training, health and safety, industrial relations and poverty (the latter affects particular groups such as the unemployed, elderly and disabled). In addition to the breadth of miscellaneous subjects covered, countries have had distinctly different national systems. These range from a liberal perspective at one extreme, preferring individual responsibility and self-help, to the opposite extreme of extensive social welfare provision and strongly egalitarian systems. The latter will be enhanced by the Scandinavian enlargement of the EU in 1995, especially by Sweden. Progress in developing social policy has been spasmodic, depending upon mobilizing sufficient support from those in favour of it, such as the Commission, the EP and trades unions, and minimizing opposition from particular employers and member states, such as the UK. For example, the UK (under a Conservative government) has made it plain that whilst agreement is possible on measures such as health and safety, it is staunchly opposed to other practices, such as works councils. This is despite the fact that where firms have plants in two or more member countries, works councils are to be created, and United Biscuits has decided to introduce these for all its workers, including those in the UK.

Health and safety measures are of long standing, dating from particularly dangerous and hazardous conditions in the coal and steel and nuclear industries. Concern with health and safety is important since there are some 8 000 deaths a year in the EU from work-related illnesses and accidents, plus the costs of health treatment for those who suffer. In the EU the approach is based upon information and regulation, whereas in the USA there is a stronger focus on insurance company compensation. Health and safety was part of the 1974 social action programme which resulted in an early Directive on the protection of workers from exposure to chemical, physical and biological agents at work, plus more specific Directives on exposure to noise and a range of toxins. Also in the mid 1970s, a committee was set up which has continued to advise the Commission on health, safety and hygiene at work.

However, most progress has been made since the SEA, which has increased the attention given to health and safety. Article 118a of the SEA paid particular attention to improvements in health and safety at work in an attempt to prevent competition driving down standards. It was recognized that special provision would be needed to prevent onerous conditions being placed on small firms. Health and safety was the first to come under qualified majority voting. Legislation for health and safety has required continuous changes and updating to keep pace with technical change. It has begun to shift away from very detailed regulation of specific workplace hazards towards the setting of more general minimum standards. The 1989 framework Directive empha- sized that the first priority was prevention of accidents, where possible through collective protection for all workers affected. This is preferable simply to accepting risks and trying to protect individual workers, for example, through issuing protective clothing. The European Court of Justice has also reached important supportive judgements. The case in 1991 of *Francovich* vs *the Italian Republic* was important since it held that even where an employer becomes insolvent, employees still have to be protected by health and safety measures and the plaintiff can claim damages, in this case from the Italian government. Employees can claim compensation if their health has been affected through the failure of governments to implement an EC health and safety Directive. The range of health and safety issues has widened to include not just compensation for occupational diseases, but also to a concern for the broader health protection of Community citizens. It goes beyond prob- lems such as shift working at night to broader social concerns such as alcoholism, drug abuse and AIDS.

Social policy took off and expanded from the early 1970s, with the initiative launched at the 1972 Paris Summit, and the proposed enlarge- ment of the EC with the entry of the UK, Ireland and Denmark. For example, Ireland was keen to see the introduction of a poverty action programme. Heads of state committed themselves both to the Commu- nity regional policy and to the social action programme. In seeking to improve living and working conditions this led to the establishment of the European Foundation for the Improvement of Living and Working Conditions, the European Institute for Vocational Training and the European Trade Union Institute. During the 1970s progress continued not just along accepted lines of enhancing health and safety and gender equality, but also in new areas: for example, Directives providing rights of information and consultation to employees in firms which were intending to declare redundancies or which were involved in a change of ownership. Unfortunately, the momentum towards stronger regional and social policies was handicapped by national recession. A slower rate of economic growth reduced the resources available for specific commitments, whilst employers tended to oppose measures which fur- ther threatened their profitability. For example, the Vredeling Directive of 1980, concerned with forcing transnational companies to inform and consult their employees on a regular basis, was stopped in its tracks.

Also, draft Directives which needed unanimity were blocked, with particularly strong opposition from the UK.

Despite attempts to resuscitate European social policy, such as that by the French Socialists in the early 1980s, the main turning point was the commitment by the Commission in the late 1980s to link the internal market to similar progress in social policy. In other words, Single Market integration was not to be an end in itself, but a means to both political and social aspirations. Whilst social policy appears to complement Single Market policy, the former involves far more intervention and regulation. These contrast with the liberalism and deregulation in many aspects of the Single Market which were approved and endorsed in the UK.

The SEA widened the scope of social policy after 1987, defining the areas to be covered by majority or unanimous voting and recognizing those topics outside its competence, such as pay, strikes and lock-outs. The Commission was given renewed responsibility for encouraging a dialogue between management and labour. New initiatives were given to improving vocational education, educational exchanges and language teaching. The Commission was less successful in other developments such as worker consultation by companies.

The principal development took place in 1989 with Commission proposals for the implementation of a Community Charter of Basic Social Rights. There were 47 initiatives grouped under various headings and these were accepted by other member states apart from the UK. Most of the basic rights laid down represent valid principles and aspirations, generally not highly contestable, but references to minimum wages and employee participation, and so on, pose particular difficulties. The Social Charter was not a legally binding document but outlined proposed developments which formed a basis for the Maastricht Treaty. New Articles 2 and 3 reconfirmed social goals in a broader and revised form. Specific concerns included movement of people, the ESF, education and training. The major innovation now is the change in emphasis from workers to citizens, with the creation of European citizenship. Citizens are able to move and reside freely, and to vote and stand as a candidate in municipal and EP elections in all member states. Citizens can also petition the EP and the European Ombudsman. Outside the EU citizens can seek diplomatic protection from the services of any member state.

The Maastricht Treaty enhances legislative action and the Council may use qualified majority voting on health and safety matters, working conditions, information and consultation of workers, gender equality and integration of persons excluded from the labour market. Unanimity applies to other issues such as social security and the protection of redundant workers, the defence and representation of workers and employers' interests, employment conditions for third country nationals, and financial contributions for promoting jobs (Collins in El-Agraa (ed.), 1994, p. 383).

Whereas the 11 member states reaffirmed their commitment to social policy, the UK opt-out will exclude British workers from many future social policy developments, though British companies operating on the continent will have to comply with EU legislation. The British opt-out contradicts the principle of non-discriminatory treatment between EU workers. However, the 11 member states have in most instances tried to get UK agreement, giving the latter more time for transition on issues such as working time and employment of young workers. Even without UK participation some divisions are now being brought out into the open between countries such as Germany and Denmark with their higher level of social protection and costs, compared with Spain, Portugal and Greece which are concerned about increased costs. Nevertheless, without the UK the poorer member states will be unable to muster sufficient blocking votes against. This means that many decisions will go ahead, with the UK gaining only a short-term respite, with the return of the Labour government leading to an acceptance of social measures including ones which the UK has been unable to influence or dilute.

From 1986–91 the main success in employment creation (compared with unassisted areas) has been in Objective 2 regions. Unfortunately, over the same period in Objective 1 and Objective 5b areas the growth in overall employment was lower than that in the unassisted areas. The main reason for this discrepancy is caused by the large share of employment in agriculture in Objectives 1 and 5b areas. Greece in particular has performed badly, partly because of such large numbers employed in agriculture, with Portugal and Spain having experienced a much better performance in job creation. Only in industry and services has job creation in the assisted areas exceeded that in the non-assisted areas. Hence unemployment has remained high, with no tendency for it to fall more than in the unassisted areas (see Figure 7.1). The sole exception is in Objective 2 areas where unemployment declined from 13 per cent in 1986 to 9.5 per cent in 1991. There has also been a significant improvement in the structure of industrial employment in Objective 2 regions towards faster-growing sectors. By contrast, in

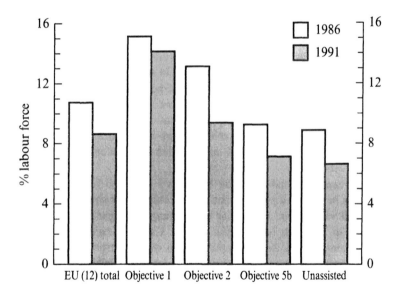

Source: Commission, Employment in Europe, 1993, p. 122.

*Figure 7.1   Unemployment rates in the Community by structural
        funds status, 1986 and 1991*

Objective 1 regions between 1986 and 1991 unemployment fell by only 1 per cent (from 15 per cent to 14 per cent) compared with a greater fall in unemployment in the non-assisted areas.

Since the main criterion used for designation of Objective 1 regions is income per head of less than 75 per cent of the EU average, let us turn to the growth rates achieved from 1986–90. In Objective 1 regions the growth rate was in fact faster at 3.5 per cent, compared with 3 per cent in the non-assisted areas (see Figures 7.2 and 7.3). The fastest economic growth was achieved in Spain, Portugal and Ireland, where there was a marked improvement compared with the previous ten years during which disparities in income per head had widened. Less satisfactory was the performance of Greece and also of the Mezzogiorno, whose growth in income per head in 1986–90 was insufficient to close the gap with northern Italy. The potential for improved economic growth in Objective 1 regions is enormous with considerable labour reserves (because of high unemployment and low activity rates). This growth

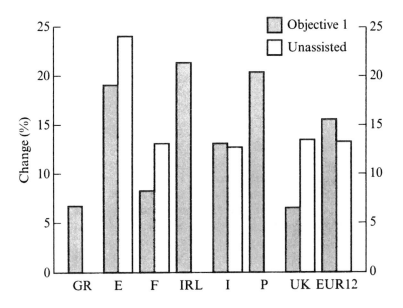

Source: Commission, Employment in Europe, 1993, p. 121.

Figure 7.2   GDP growth in Objective 1 and unassisted regions, 1986–90

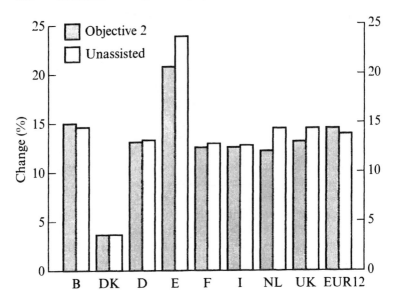

Source: Commission, Employment in Europe, 1993, p. 121.

*Figure 7.3   GDP growth in Objective 2 and unassisted regions,
1986–90*

has been constrained by overdependence on agriculture, and an industrial structure which comprises a high proportion of low growth industries. A partial exception to the latter is Ireland which has attracted
inward investment of high technology firms.

There has been a marked improvement in economic growth in Objective 1 regions brought about by the additional injections of investment and the effects have been confirmed through the macroeconomic
models used to assess the impact of assistance under the CSF (CEC,
1992, pp. 113–14). One can expect this to continue with the increased
concentration in structural fund expenditure on these regions during the
1990s. Unfortunately this has not been reflected to the same degree of
success in reducing unemployment, apart from in Portugal where the
CSF was expected to create about 70,000 new jobs 1989–93 and unemployment is low. The effect on employment for Greece was small, with
an increase in employment of just over 45,000 predicted 1989–93,

whilst in Spain extra job creation of nearly 120,000 over the five years clearly made little impact on its heavy unemployment total.

In the author's view, the lack of success in reducing unemployment constitutes a major failing, but other writers choose to focus narrowly on aspects in which at first sight the structural funds have been successful. For example, Scott (1995) examines the economic growth which has been achieved but is not content with the way this has been measured by economists through the use of GDP figures. She would prefer less emphasis to be placed by the EU on GDP statistics in favour of a broader qualitative measure or, if a quantified measure is to be used, would choose a Physical Quality of Life Index which covers life expectancy, infant mortality and literacy; or a Human Development Index covering longevity, educational attainment and real per capita GDP. Scott concludes that an Index of Sustainable Economic Welfare is a radically better alternative than GDP in measuring quality of life.

At heart, Scott seems to have latched on to an anti-growth environmental band wagon, rejecting the notion of economic growth 'trickling down to those most in need'. Despite the representation of EU policymakers that its regional policy is consistent with its environmental policy through its environmental impact assessments, the reality is that these are subservient to the over-riding philosophy of achieving economic regional growth. Member states, in submitting their CSFs, confirm that these conform with EU environmental rules; but the move away from detailed submission of projects to programmes makes it difficult to examine the impact of individual projects and their cumulative effect. Scott favours widening the basis of the Monitoring Committees to include representatives of environmental interest groups, though she recognizes the potential for greater delays and added bureaucracy which would arise from this.

The next section goes on to examine some of the factors limiting the effectiveness of the structural funds. These comprise: national expenditure cutbacks; structural fund expenditure still modest, partly because of the limited size of the EU budget; EAGGF expenditure dominated by guarantee spending; the growth of regional problems, including the eastern *Länder* of Germany; the difficulty in ensuring additionality of structural fund expenditure; overemphasis on infrastructure and insufficient productive investment; and ESF expenditure, whilst beneficial, only providing the preconditions for growth, which ultimately can only come from a major increase in demand-side expenditure in the economy. For the UK the switch of funding from the poor to the poorest regions in the EU means that the structural funds alone offer no panacea to its regional problems.

ELEMENTS CONSTRAINING SUCCESS

The key issue is the financial resources which have been mobilized both by the member states and the EU, and whether these are sufficient to tackle the magnitude of the growing regional problems brought about by enlargement. The effects of national regional policy expenditure are particularly important, and in the early 1980s national governmental expenditure on regional policy was estimated to be more than five times that of the ERDF (Vanhove and Klaassen, 1987, p. 474). National regional policy has a long history in the UK and Italy, but after many years application has failed to close the north–south divide in either country. This may be partly because surveys interviewing firms on the value of regional aid show that although it has been helpful, many firms placed regional aid low in comparison with the need for other crucially competitive factors to be in place (Artis and Lee (eds), 1994, p. 189). Nevertheless, any failings of national regional policies in the past are unlikely to be remedied by deep expenditure cutbacks.

However, national governments, given their tightening budgetary constraints and changing priorities, have felt themselves forced to prune their own regional policies. In the case of the UK, regional policy expenditure fell from £1 558 million in 1978–79 to £738 million in 1988–89, a fall of just over half in the decade. This was only offset partially by an increase in expenditure on urban policy from £388 million in 1979–80 to £750 million in 1989–90 (Day and Rees (eds), 1994, p. 168). For example, in the search for greater cost-effectiveness, many countries have moved from automatic to more discretionary financial incentives; these include the UK particularly, and also France, Spain and Germany. An aim of this discretionary change has been to try and target aid to projects which would not otherwise be developed. Given the relative failure of national regional policies to solve the problem of imbalance and expenditure cutbacks, why should we expect any greater success from increasing EU expenditure on this?

Structural fund outlays have risen significantly and now account for a third of the budget, increasing to 35–40 per cent of the budget by 1999, equivalent to almost half a per cent of EU GDP. The increase in the scale of the regional funds is welcomed by many and is needed not only to offset the cutbacks in national expenditure, but also to come to terms with the magnitude of unemployment nationally which has spread to nearly all regions. EU problems have been aggravated by southern enlargement and the vast amount of investment needed, particularly in infrastructure, to increase the level of development. Padoa-Schioppa *et al.* (1987) calculated that for a 1 per cent increase in GDP, gross investment in less favoured regions would need to increase by ECU 55–76 billion: the former figure was based on the marginal efficiency of investment (MEI) being the same as in the country as a whole, and the latter figure using a lower MEI in the region than in the country overall. They also estimated that to create 1.5 million jobs through direct productive investment (assuming one job cost ECU 50,000) would cost ECU 75 billion, that is, ECU 15 billion a year (Padoa-Schioppa *et al.* 1987, p. 171).

The EU would have the resources to finance this level of expenditure if the benefits of the SEM materialize. For example, the gains were estimated at around ECU 216 billion for the EC (12) at 1988 prices (Cecchini, 1988). These may be considered an overestimate if one believes they exaggerate potential gains from increased economies of scale and so on, or an underestimate if one expects even more beneficial dynamic effects on investment. If one takes the Cecchini figures as the best available until the new post-1992 impact studies are conducted, it can be seen that structural fund expenditure is still relatively small compared with the projected gains of 5.3 per cent of GDP from the Single Market. For example, the total budget will rise to only 1.27 per cent of GDP. Also, the whole structural spending over six years up to 1999 of ECU 141.48 billion is still far short of the projected Single Market benefits. Therefore it can be concluded that the structural fund expenditure is still not sufficient in relation to current structural problems, which will grow even further if the EU widens to include much of eastern Europe.

There is also the issue beyond total expenditure to a consideration of the way it has been spent. Certainly more concentration of expenditure on those in greatest need is desirable on equity grounds and is likely to produce greater effects. However, it should be remembered that neither the EAGGF nor the ESF were devised to deal with regional problems. In fact, the EAGGF has actually added to the problem of regional imbalance through its guaranteed price expenditure, and other EU policies have also tended to have detrimental effects on weaker regions.

The adverse effects of such policies have been established in various studies (Molle and Cappellin (eds), 1988). The attempt to bring about greater synergy between the three structural funds: the ERDF, the ESF and the EAGGF, assisted by the EIB, is clearly desirable. However, there are social field elements within the Social Charter which are actually inimical to the process of job creation, especially in SMEs. Yet it is recognized that indigenous development by the latter now constitutes the key to successful regional development, as so many areas compete for a diminishing share of inward multinational investment.

In the past, EU member states have all expected to receive something from the ERDF and in this can be likened, for example, to the British welfare system in which everybody believes that they are entitled to some return for their contributions. Despite the attempts to diminish ERDF expenditure to those countries which do not really need it, Germany, for example, now has the eastern *Länder* to support. After re-unification a development plan was put forward and a CSF (1991–93) agreed for the following: East Berlin, Mecklenburg-Vorpommern, Brandenburg, Sachsen-Anhalt, Thuringen and Sachsen. ECU 3 billion was set aside for this, with spending at ECU 1 billion per annum. It was split between ECU 1 500 million through the ERDF, ECU 900 million through the ESF and ECU 600 million through the EAGGF. Over the period 1994–99 EU funding has doubled to about ECU 2 billion per annum to the new *Länder*.

The UK, with its slower relative economic growth, now has three Objective 1 regions (in addition to its traditional concern with Objective 2 regions). Everybody is lobbying strongly, from member states downwards to separate regions and groups of regions seeking to influence the Commission. For example, regions in the UK dependent on coalmining helped to create the Rechar initiative. The British government supported this since it brought in beneficial funding. Enlargement of the EU in the future is likely to involve not just increased regional spending for poor east European countries: even the rich EFTA countries which joined the EU in 1995 have had their sparsely populated regions considered under a new Objective 6 status (Hooghe and Keating, 1994). This relates to sparsely populated regions (below eight inhabitants per square kilometre). The biggest beneficiary is Finland with 16.7 per cent of its national population covered by Objectives 1 and 6, compared with 5.25 per cent for Sweden and 3.5 per cent for Austria.

There have been major delays in the implementation of policy which have affected the UK, especially in its Objective 2 areas. Arguments over the definition of such areas have caused uncertainty in funding for potential applicants. For the UK, the structural funds *per se* offer no panacea to its problems. This is not only because it is a minor recipient from the EAGGF, but also because the redesignation of EU regional problems has switched emphasis from the poor UK regions to even poorer ones elsewhere. Some indication of the UK's decline at a national level is shown by the fact that Germany is well above the UK in GDP per capita even after the inclusion of its eastern *Länder*, and Italy is also better off than the UK because of the wealth of the northern regions. In France, even the poorest area, Nord Pas de Calais, is wealthier than the majority of British regions. Even if one focuses on non-economic indicators such as health, the UK fares poorly, with the highest rate of heart disease in the EU and the second highest death rate from cancer.

A further point to bear in mind in assessing the effects of structural funds is the extent to which these have really constituted additionality. They are supposed to be additional, promoting spending for specific purposes which the recipient would not have undertaken in the absence of a grant. Unfortunately, in some instances they have substituted for national government expenditure, going into general government funds. Although this fulfils a redistributive function at least for the poorest member states, its resource allocation effect is lost. Since the money is disbursed via national governments, it has been tempting for them to replace their own funding by EU funding. Whilst the movement towards financing programmes rather than projects is to be welcomed generally, this broad expenditure made structural funding fairly fungible with other types of spending. Some poorer countries, such as Greece, have found it difficult to provide matching funding, and have also regarded the EU structural funds more as a national budgetary transfer than a valuable means to promote regional development. Both the ERDF and ESF have been open to criticism, with the latter also taken to task on the issue of additionality which applied mainly to the very small percentage of its expenditure on innovatory social developments.

The revised regulations of the structural funds have emphasized that these must be additional and may not replace public expenditure on structural expenditure: the member state has to retain its expenditure at the same level as before. This is vital and some would like to see the conditions underlying structural funding tightened even further, perhaps through adopting a similar approach to that of the Cohesion Fund in tying the funding more conditionally to macroeconomic performance. However, not everyone would agree with further EU encroachment on national economic sovereignty and the author remains unconvinced by any call for further deflationary measures.

Many are also critical of the focus of EU expenditure, which has been mainly through making improvements to the operation of a market system, rather than extensive direct investment. For example, the EU has not used any physical controls to try to curb expansion in core regions and indeed national governments have also retreated from such measures. Instead, EU regional policy has been wedded strongly to investment in infrastructure, particularly in Objective 1 regions. Infrastructure expenditure prior to 1987 was about 80 per cent of regional expenditure. One can agree that there is a close correlation between infrastructure and level of economic development, but the question is: which is the causal factor? Infrastructure tackles bottlenecks and facilitates the movement of goods and services not only out of regions but into them as well. Furthermore, moves towards privatization in infrastructure, such as transport and telecommunications, will reduce the scope for cross-subsidization for provision in peripheral regions. The EU continues its concern for infrastructure spending in the Cohesion Fund, though infrastructure has now become more widely defined. New plans to diminish the percentage of ERDF infrastructure investment are desirable and in future 40 per cent of Objective 1 expenditure and 80 per cent of Objective 2 expenditure is to be targeted on productive investment.

The EU finances hard infrastructure investment through the ERDF and the Cohesion Fund, whilst the ESF has focused on soft infrastructure investment to improve education and training. This is poor in southern Europe, with the percentage of young people between 16 and 18 years of age receiving education and training being as low as 38 per cent in Portugal, 53 per cent in Spain, 59 per cent in Greece and also only 60 per cent in the UK (Holland, 1993). The latter has problems at all levels with relatively low educational attainment and insufficient practical work in schools. After school there is also a lack of apprenticeships, though National Vocational Qualifications are a step forward and place great emphasis on competencies. An increase in British training levels and standards towards German levels, such as that of the skilled German foreman (*Meister*), would help to plug the major productivity gap which applies in most sectors between the two economies. Certainly the main problem, especially in Objective 2 regions, is not hard infrastructure but the problem of outdated skills in many industries which require retraining. ESF expenditure has financed all types of training, especially vocational training which in some years has received over four-fifths of expenditure. This has left only a small amount of expenditure for recruitment subsidies, wage subsidies and vocational guidance (Cutler *et al.*, 1989, p. 82).

The assumption is that better vocational training and lifetime education will rebuild long-term competitiveness by moving regions into high productivity knowledge-based industries. It is into these higher value-added sectors that the EU needs to move its resources, leaving most of the down-market sectors to the NICs. The emphasis on education and training has been reflected in the various regional plans submitted, such as in the UK's Merseyside 2000 Plan which proposed to devote 44 per cent of expenditure to the ESF (with the remaining 56 per cent to the ERDF).

The EU, through the ESF, has provided valuable support in improving and underpinning education and training systems, particularly in less developed regions. It has also made many of these regions more aware of the needs of those less qualified and most vulnerable to unemployment. Nevertheless, deficiencies still remain. For example, Cutler *et al.* (1989, p. 85) in the UK have shown that most of the YTS places were found in service sectors, perhaps indicating that de-industrialization has reached such a critical level that retraining is insufficient to regenerate British industry. However, if the future lies mainly with the service sector, then clearly training has to match the vacancies which exist. Currently high unemployment is suppressing the skill shortages which are likely to emerge once firms start to recruit again for unfilled vacancies. Education and training provide valuable long-term investment in human capital, but unfortunately in the short run in many parts of the EU qualifications have grown faster than the jobs which require them. At the present time (1995) what is mainly visible is a better educated dole queue, and the real hope is that policies in the EU can engineer a major economic recovery.

Bibliography

Albrechts, L. *et al.* (1989), *Regional Policy at the Crossroads: European Perspectives*, London: Jessica Kingsley.

Ardagh, J. (1982), *France in the 1980s*, Harmondsworth: Penguin.

Armstrong, H. and Taylor, J. (1985), *Regional Economics and Policy*, Oxford: Philip Allan.

Armstrong, H., Taylor, J. and Williams, A. (1994), 'Regional Policy', in Artis, M.J. and Lee, N. (eds), *The Economics of the European Union*, Oxford: Oxford University Press.

Artis, M.J. and Lee, N. (eds) (1994), *The Economics of the European Union*, Oxford: Oxford University Press.

Bacon, R. and Eltis, W. (1976), *Britain's Economic Problem – Too Few Producers*, London: Macmillan, 2nd edition.

Bliss, C. and Braga de Macedo, J. (1990), *Unity with Diversity in the European Economy: The Community's Southern Frontier*, Cambridge: Cambridge University Press.

Boltho, A. (1989), 'European and United States Income Differentials: A Note', *Oxford Review of Economic Policy*, 5 (2), 105–15.

Borner, S. and Grubel, H. (1992), *The European Community after 1992*, London: Macmillan.

Cecchini, P. (1988), *The European Challenge: The Benefit of a Single Market*, Aldershot: Wildwood House, Gower.

Centre for European Policy Studies (1992), *The Annual Review of Community Affairs 1991*, London: Brassey's

Coffey, P. (1995), *The Future of Europe*, Aldershot: Edward Elgar.

Commission of the European Communities (1973), *Thomson Report on the Regional Problem in the Enlarged Community*, 550 Final, Brussels.

Commission of the European Communities (1977), *McDougall Report of the Study Group on the Role of Public Finance in European Integration*, Brussels.

Commission of the European Communities (1989), 'Economic Convergence in the Community', *European Economy*, No. 41, Brussels.

Commission of the European Communities (1991a), *Employment in Europe*, 248 Final, Brussels.

Commission of the European Communities (1991b), 'Social Europe', *The European Social Fund*, No. 2, Brussels.

Commission of the European Communities (1992), *Second Annual Report on the Implementation of the Reform of the Structural Funds*, Brussels.

Commission of the European Communities (1993a), *Trade and Foreign Investment in the Community's Regions: The Impact of Economic Reform in Central and Eastern Europe*, No. 7, Brussels.

Commission of the European Communities (1993b), *New Location Factors for Mobile Investment in Europe*, Final Report No. 6, Brussels.

Commission of the European Communities (1993c), *Community Structural Funds 1994–99 – Revised Regulations and Comments*, Brussels.

Commission of the European Communities (1993d), 'Stable Money Sound Finances', *European Economy*, No. 53, Brussels.

Commission of the European Communities (1993e), Green Paper, *European Social Policy*, 551, Brussels.

Commission of the European Communities (1994a), 'Growth and Employment', *European Economy*, No. 1, Brussels.

Commission of the European Communities (1994b), 'EC Agricultural Policy for the 21st Century', *European Economy*, No. 4, Brussels.

Commission of the European Communities (1994c), *The Agricultural Situation in the Community in 1993*, Brussels.

Commission of the European Communities (1994d), *Growth, Competitiveness, Employment*, White Paper, Brussels.

Commission of the European Communities (1994e), *Eurostat: Basic Statistics of the Community*, Luxembourg.

Commission of the European Communities (1994f), *Employment in Europe*.

Commission of the European Communities (1995), *Finance from Europe* (compiled by M. Hopkins, Loughborough, for the Representation of the European Commission in the UK).

Cutler, T. *et al.* (1989), *1992 – The Struggle for Europe*, Oxford: Berg.

Davidson, A. and Seary, B. (1990), *Grants from Europe*, 6th edition, London: Bedford Square Press.

Dawson, A.H. (1993), *A Geography of European Integration*, London: Belhaven.

Day, G. and Rees, G. (eds) (1994), *Regions, Nations and European Integration*, Cardiff: University of Wales.

Drèze, J. (1993), 'Regions of Europe: A Feasible Status to be Discussed', *Economic Policy*, No. 17, October, 265–307.

EIB Annual Reports: EIB Information 1990–94, Luxembourg.

El-Agraa, A.M. (ed.) (1994), *The Economics of the European Community*, 4th edition, Hemel Hempstead: Harvester Wheatsheaf.

Elliot, R.F. (1991), *Labor Economics: A Comparative Text*, Maidenhead: McGraw-Hill.

Gravier, J.F. (1947), *Paris et le Désert Français*, Paris: Flammarion.

Gros, D. and Thygesen, N. (1992), *European Monetary Integration*, Harlow: Longman.

Hall, P. (1981), 'Cycles of Innovation: The Geography of the Fifth Kondratieff Cycle', *New Society*, **55** (958), 535–7.

Hall, P. (1989), *Urban and Regional Planning*, London: Unwin/Hyman.

Hannequart, A. (ed.) (1992), *Economic and Social Cohesion in Europe*, London: Routledge.

Harris, L. (1985), 'Long Waves in Economic Life', *D210 Introduction to Economics*, Unit 1, Milton Keynes: Open University.

Harrop, J. (1978a), 'The European Investment Bank', *National Westminster Bank Quarterly Review*, May, 18–26.

Harrop, J. (1978b), 'An Evaluation of the European Investment Bank', *Societé Universitaire Européenne de Recherche Financière*, 23a Tilburg, Netherlands.

Harrop, J. (1985), 'Crisis in the Machine Tool Industry: A Policy Dilemma for the European Community', *Journal of Common Market Studies*, **XXIV** (1), September, 61–75.

Harrop, J. (1992), *The Political Economy of Integration in the European Community*, 2nd edition, Aldershot: Edward Elgar.

Harrop, J. (1994), 'The Role of Tourism in the European Community', *European Business Review*, **94** (2), 20–25.

Harvey, C. (1994), *The Rise of Regional Europe*, London: Pinter.

Henderson, R. (1993), *European Finance*, Maidenhead: McGraw-Hill.

Hitiris, T. (1988), *European Community Economics*, Hemel Hempstead: Harvester Wheatsheaf.

Holland, S. (1976a), *The Regional Problem*, Basingstoke: Macmillan.

Holland, S. (1976b), *Capital Versus the Regions*, Basingstoke: Macmillan.

Holland, S. (1979), *The State as Entrepreneur*, London: Weidenfeld and Nicolson.

Holland, S. (1993), *The European Imperative*, Nottingham: Spokesman.

Hooghe, L. and Keating, M. (1994), 'The Politics of European Union Regional Policy', *Journal of European Public Policy*, **3** (1), 367–93.

Italianer, A. and Van Heukelen, M. (1993), 'Proposals for Community Stabilization Mechanisms: Some Historical Applications', *The Economics of Community Public Finance, European Economy*, No. 5, 1993.

Kaldor, N. (1966), *Causes of the Slow Rate of Growth of the UK Economy*, Cambridge: Cambridge University Press.

Keating, M. and Jones, B. (1985), *Regions in the Community*, Oxford: Clarendon Press.

Leonardi, R. (ed.) (1993), *The Regions and the European Community*, London: Frank Cass.

Lewis, J. and Townsend, A. (eds) (1989), *The North–South Divide*, London: Paul Chapman Publishing.

Lloyds Bank (1994), 'The Future of Farming', *Bulletin*, No. 185, May, London: Lloyds Bank.

Mair, D. (1991), 'Regional Policy Initiatives', *The Royal Bank of Scotland Review*, No. 169, March, 33–43.

Marsden, D.W. (ed.) 1992, *Pay and Employment in the New Europe*, Aldershot: Edward Elgar.

Marshall, M. (1987), *Long Waves of Regional Development*, Basingstoke: Macmillan.

Massey, D. and Allen, J. (eds) (1988), *Uneven Redevelopment*, London: Hodder and Stoughton in association with the Open University.

McAleavy, P. and Mitchell, J. (1994), 'Industrial Regions and Lobbying in the Structural Funds Reforms Process', *Journal of Common Market Studies*, **32** (2), June, 237–48.

Mensch, G. (1979), *Stalemate in Technology*, New York: Ballinger.

Michie, J. and Grieve Smith, J. (eds) (1994), *Unemployment in Europe*, London Academic Press.

Molle, W. (1990), *The Economics of European Integration*, Aldershot: Dartmouth.

Molle, W. and Cappellin, R. (eds) (1988), *Regional Impact of Community Policies in Europe*, Aldershot: Avebury.

Neilsen, J.U.M. *et al.* (1991), *An Economic Analysis of the EC*, Maidenhead: McGraw-Hill.

Nevin, E. (1990), *The Economics of Europe*, London: Macmillan.

Padoa-Schioppa, T. *et al.* (1987), *Efficiency, Stability and Equity*, Oxford: Oxford University Press.

Pearce, D. (1987), *Tourism Today: A Geographical Analysis*, Harlow: Longman.

Redmond, J. (1993), *The Next Mediterranean Enlargement of the European Community: Turkey, Cyprus and Malta*, Aldershot: Dartmouth.

Ross, J.F. (1994), 'High-Speed Rail: Catalyst for European Integration?', *Journal of Common Market Studies*, **32** (2), June, 191–214.

Schaefer, G. (1993), 'Regions in the Policy Process of the EC – Reflections on the Innovations of the Maastricht Treaty', *Eipascope*, European Journal of Public Administration, No. 3, Maastricht, Netherlands, 8–10.

Schumpeter, J.A. (1939), *Business Cycles*, New York: McGraw Hill.

Scott, J. (1995), *Development Dilemmas in the European Community*, Buckingham: Open University.

Tsoukalis, L. (1993), *The New European Economy*, 2nd edition, Oxford: Oxford University Press.

Vanhove, N. and Klaassen, H. (1987), *Regional Policy: A European Approach*, 2nd edition, Aldershot: Gower.

Vickerman, R. (1992), *The Single European Market*, Hemel Hempstead: Harvester Wheatsheaf.

Wildavsky, A. and Zapico-Goni, E. (eds) (1993), *National Budgeting for Economic and Monetary Union*, Netherlands: Martinus Nijhoff.

Williams, A.M. (1994), *The European Community: The Contradictions of Integration*, 2nd edition, Oxford: Blackwell.

Wise, M. and Gibb, R. (1993), *Single Market to Social Europe*, Harlow: Longman.

Yuill, D., Allen, K. and Hull, C. (eds) (1980), *Regional Policy in the European Community*, London: Croom Helm.

Index